GOD CRIED AT AUSCHWITZ

To James Van Praagh.

To Love unconditionally is spiritual fulfillment. Thank you for illuminating The Way so clearly —

Loving Best wishes

Betty Lissiac

Tel. 9398-1975

This book is dedicated to my children, grandchildren
and all those loved ones who did not make it home.
I wrote this for you.

GOD CRIED AT AUSCHWITZ

The journey within

BETTY LISSING

2/18 Dainty Crescent
Randwick 2031 Sydney

First published in 2003 by LMN Systems Pty Ltd

Edited by Emma Cotter
Design and production by GTG Pty Limited
Printed by Griffin Press, Adelaide

National Library of Australia
Cataloguing-in-publication data

Lissing, Rebecca, 1923- .
God cried at Auschwitz : the journey within.

ISBN 0 646 42243 X.

1. Lissing, Rebecca, 1923- .
2. Auschwitz (Concentration camp).
3. Holocaust survivors - Biography. I. Title.

940.5318092

www.godcried.com.au

PREFACE

It would be impossible to calculate how many books have been written by survivors of the Holocaust. In fact, one extremely cynical publisher went so far as to say that in many cases you could just change the name of the author and have the same book.

But not this one.

Betty Lissing is a remarkable woman, who, within these pages, embarks upon a spiritual journey which, without the horrors of Auschwitz, she could never have begun. Oh yes, she describes the pain and degradation as Hitler's Third Reich attempted to change her from a human being into a number but, in Betty's case, it didn't work.

The brutal dehumanisation she experienced becomes a voyage of self-discovery and slowly develops into an amazing philosophy of forgiveness and hope for the future of mankind. Nowhere is there even a trace of self-pity. Every experience is placed in a context of quiet resignation, tolerance and amazing forgiveness.

That Betty not only survived her journey but has captured the subtle nuances of her gradual spiritual evolvement is all the more remarkable because Betty writes in English, although her native tongue is Dutch.

As many eminent authors have written, it is essential that the memories of what happened within the barbed-wire confines of the death camps never be forgotten. It is also essential that we realise and wonderingly appreciate that even there, the human spirit could rise above the hatred and desolation to still find something beautiful within the human condition—and beyond.

This book is both challenging and inspiring.

There are far too few Betty Lissings.

Roger Climpson

ACKNOWLEDGEMENTS

This is the true story of my experiences during the Second World War and the events that took place after my capture by the Gestapo.

It is the story of my liberation, and reunion with my husband, Herman Lissing, while I was a patient at Castle Eerde in Ommen.

It is also the story of my inner journey in the pursuit of peace and a meaningful existence on this Earthly plane.

My heartfelt thanks to Roger Climpson, for writing the Preface to my story. Roger is the author of *Elinda*, and has always had a real perception of our individual outlook in our struggle to survive the memories of our past.

I also send loving thoughts to the late Shula Rovkin, who persuaded me to commit my story to paper, and to her sister Ruth, for finishing the job of typing the manuscript.

My deepest gratitude to Joel Goldsmith and Lorraine Sinkler for illuminating the way so clearly.

My grateful thanks to Emma Cotter, who did a wonderful job in editing my book, and to Bruno Jean Grasswill, who has been in charge of the layout and design of the book and its cover—without them I could not have finished it.

CONTENTS

FOREWORD

It was more than fifty years after my liberation from the hell of Auschwitz when I came to the shock realisation that indeed God cried at Auschwitz.

When people find out that I am a survivor of the Holocaust, the question most frequently put to me is 'Where was God at Auschwitz?' How, if there is a God, could He have tolerated the death camps and allowed the slaughter of millions of innocent people, their lives snuffed out by the murderous rampage of the Nazi regime?

Even the victims, while on their final journey, could not comprehend the enormity of the crime that was about to destroy them. When they came face to face with the annihilation of their existence on this earth, it was too late for mothers to save their children, for husbands to save their wives, or for children to save their parents from a gruesome death.

As a survivor of Auschwitz, it still remains a mystery to me how this diabolical plan for the total destruction of an entire people, simply because of their Jewish faith, could be carried out.

I was born and raised in the Netherlands. So was my entire family, which can be traced back for over 300 years in the Netherlands. I had the good fortune to be born into a civilised and cultured society that respected the individual's right to be whatever they chose, provided they did not infringe on the right of others to practise their way of life.

On May 10, 1940, our peace-loving life was violated. Like thieves in the night, the Germans invaded the Netherlands, in order to indulge their desire to teach us their grotesque plan for race purification.

It did not take long for our population to descend into decline, as the occupying forces plundered and looted their possessions and food supplies, and put people into slave labour camps both in Holland and Germany. However, the Nazis had other plans for the Jewish population, which would result in the deportation of 105,000 Jewish people. Less than 5000 would return from the death camps. The rest were eliminated, among them my entire family. The Gypsies, too, were also deemed to be inferior and were deported to Auschwitz for destruction.

The madness that motivated these racists to act in such an abhorrent manner still baffles the human mind. The process of so–called race purification would cost millions of Germans their lives. Today we know that the so–called invincible leaders of that regime took poison or put a bullet through their brains, as the Allied Forces marched on Berlin. They even murdered their own wives and children when defeat was certain.

Over the long years since the liberation, I have heard all sorts of theories as to why the Jewish people were singled out for such persecution and destruction. The most infamous one seems to be that we do not accept Jesus Christ as God. How can that theory stand? Millions of European Christians were also slaughtered in the same war, in spite of their Christian faith in Jesus Christ as God.

I have since learned that humanity must realise a deeper truth, and that is this: unless we acknowledge the one Fatherhood of God for all people, we have no common cause for being on Earth and fulfilling our destiny of the brotherhood of man. There is no God enthroned in the sky or hanging on a cross. God resides in man in His fullness, but man has to make that connection and acknowledge it for Him to function in our individual lives.

So God is present at all times within man, but we have the choice of exercising our free will – to ignore or accept Him within us, in accordance with our own beliefs.

I now know that God was present at Auschwitz, and when man exercised his destructive free will, He indeed cried.

Betty Lissing

INTRODUCTION

It is 53 years since I first came to Australia from my native Holland; a move prompted by the traumas of the Second World War. My husband, Herman, and our three-year-old son, Martin, were all that was left of my immediate family – the rest had been killed in the maelstrom of the Nazi occupation.

We had found it impossible to make a new start after our liberation from the death camps, surrounded as we were by ghosts, and a friend of Herman's, a high-ranking Naval officer who had been stationed in Australia during the war, convinced us that Sydney would be a good place to settle. Herman had applied to the Australian Embassy in the Hague and we were soon accepted as settlers. We weren't migrants as such: we had a perfectly good nationality and homeland of our own, and we weren't eligible for the migrants' waiting list. As new settlers, we had to pay our own fares, and Herman had to journey on ahead of us to find himself a job and arrange accommodation for me and Martin.

It didn't take Herman long to fulfil all the bureaucratic requirements and, only three months after he had left, Martin and I were on our way. Our six weeks' voyage would put me off travelling by sea for life. Let me just say that our living conditions were basic. On Australia Day in 1950, however, we landed in Port Philip Bay. Ironically, the public holiday meant that we all had to remain on board for an extra day as there were no services running!

Suddenly, I heard my name over the loudspeaker system, summoning me to the deck. When I got there, everyone was pointing to a little rowing boat rocking on the swell, with its two passengers waving a placard with my name on it. It was Herman, who had travelled from Sydney to collect us, only to find out on his arrival that we would not be able to leave the ship. All we could do was shout our greetings to one another, before Herman had to return to Melbourne.

The next morning, he was the first on board, arriving even before the Quarantine Officers, who had to clear us for disembarkation. We stayed the night in Port Philip before catching the train to Sydney the following morning. I remember wondering if that train journey was ever going to end – it was so hot! This was my introduction to the vastness of Australia. In Holland, a couple of hours' drive in any direction would bring you to the border and I remember asking at one stage, 'Herman, are we still in Australia?'

When we arrived in Sydney, we took a taxi to Rushcutters Bay, where Herman had managed to rent a large room with a kitchenette and bathroom. As I gazed over the beautiful surroundings of the harbour, something clicked inside me. For the first time in many years, I felt at peace; something about our new home just seemed right.

Herman had found work as an interpreter and accounts clerk, and further supplemented our income by playing the piano three nights a week at the 'California Club' in Kings Cross. I enrolled Martin in the local kindergarten, where it seemed like no time at all before he was chattering away in English. For my part, I was determined to push the horrors of the war years to the back of my mind and make the most of my new life. For a while, Herman and I succeeded in suppressing our memories of our imprisonment and torture.

We began to save some money and bought a small car. Every weekend we would explore Sydney and its suburbs, sometimes driving as far as the Blue Mountains. When Martin was 6 years old, we decided it was time to have another baby, and I duly gave birth to Jack Monty, whom Martin would immediately dub 'Jerry'.

Our lives finally seemed to be running smoothly again but, some ten years after we were liberated, the horrors of the death camps came back to haunt us again. The nightmares were never-ending. I became very run down, and there seemed to be nothing that I could do to stop my memories playing themselves out over and over again in my mind. The sorrow of losing my beloved family and so many of my friends in such a way threatened to overcome me. This time, however, I knew that I could no longer push these memories to the back of my mind, and I prayed for many hours for the strength to bear my grief. It was in this weakened state that I fell pregnant with our third child, a pregnancy that would be difficult from beginning to end.

I was not to know then what I know now, that the birth of our daughter, Elinda, would change our lives for ever. This was when my journey really began, my journey within. My experiences during the war had tested my physical and mental endurance to its limits, but Elinda's birth would push me over the edge, into the inner dimension. I hope that this story, *God Cried at Auschwitz,* will show the reader how and why this child revealed to me a whole new dimension to my life, how she enabled me to climb the road to inner peace and achieve a purposeful existence on this Earth, despite the incredible horrors of the war years.

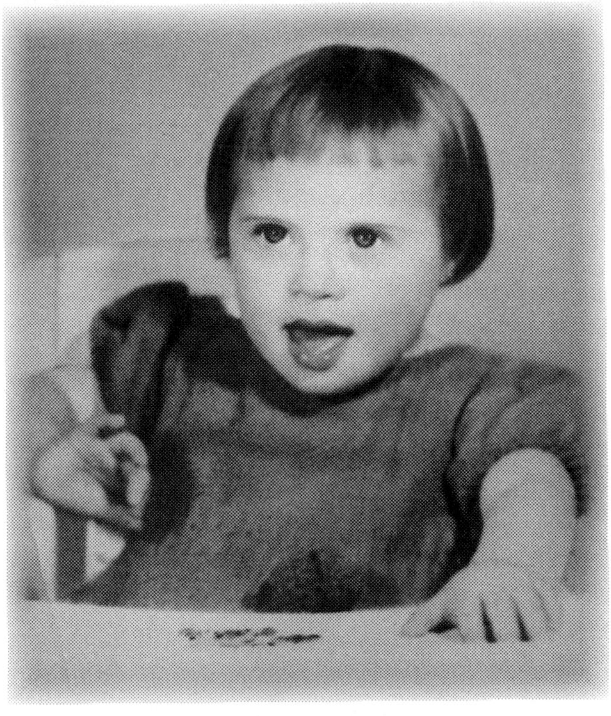

Elinda, when she was 4 years old.

My mother, Celine, with Maurits and me, 1928.

PART ONE

CHAPTER ONE

OUR FATE IS SEALED

It is difficult to explain why I burst into tears when my father told us that war had broken out. I was only 17 years old at that time and had always had the best of life, so the only way I can explain it now is that I must have had a premonition of what was to happen to all of us.

When I reflect on my childhood, I often think of the afternoon when I came home from school to find my parents huddled before the radio in our living room. There was a sense of nervous anticipation in the air. I felt that they were waiting for something important, but I had no idea what it was. One look at their faces made me stop in my tracks. I waited for them to tell me what they were expecting to hear.

Suddenly my father's face turned ashen as the radio commentator announced that Hitler had swept to power in Germany. I knew nothing about politics, but it was as if an iron fist clamped around my heart. The whole room felt cold.

It was 1933 and I was ten years old.

I overheard my family discussing the issues, but when we children were present they made light of the situation in Germany. After Hitler's regime came to power there was an immediate exodus of Jews and political opponents of the Nazis from Germany. My grandparents opened their home to refugees and for a number of years were host to an on–going stream of people fleeing the Nazis.

Most Dutch people did not expect the Germans to invade the Netherlands. Holland had remained neutral during the First World War and our government had no intention of becoming involved in another war. Nevertheless, there was a sense of foreboding in the air

Louis at school, aged about 10. He was killed on arrival in Auschwitz in December 1942.

whenever political news was discussed, or when the pogroms against the Jewish people were reported in the newspapers.

Being very young I did not dwell on such matters. But I could not shake off the feeling of doom that had overcome me when I saw the expression on my parents' faces as they listened to the announcement of Hitler's victorious *Putz*.

Holland's avowed neutrality did not prevent the Germans from invading our small country and bombing our cities into surrender. The Dutch people were in a state of shock. Our government went into exile in England, and the Royal Family also fled to England, where Queen Wilhelmina would stay for the duration of the war.

The Dutch population was trapped between the North Sea and German Occupied Europe. After the Nazis introduced slave labour to fuel their war machine, most of our young men were taken from their homes and transported to Germany.

It was a great struggle to live a free life and the general population suffered severe hardship, but it was the annihilation of its Jewish population that most shook the nation after the war, when the final murderous count was revealed.

Mother was only 42 and Father two years older, when Hitler's Germany invaded our cultured fatherland. My elder brother Maurits was 19 years old, and Louis, whom we called our 'little brother', was only 11 years old. We were a happy, average family, by no means rich, but we were never short of anything necessary for our neat, orderly life.

I was always a sports girl at heart. From the age of ten I had belonged to a well-known gymnastic club in Amsterdam, the Bato Club. I spent all my free time practising my skills. I was told I was a natural gymnast, but to me it was my great love. I went on to win the yearly club championship for the next five years, and at fifteen I won a place on the national team. Our coach was the famous Gerrit Kleerekoper, a greatly respected identity. Every morning Holland awoke to his fitness programme on the radio.

Members of the Bato Club at the beach in North Holland in 1938.
Betty is fourth from the left.

I was the official flag bearer for the Bato Club. This photo was taken at an Olympic Day March in 1937.

I think with gratitude of these years of sportsmanship. Not only was my youth a happy time of joy and fellowship, but I am convinced that my years of training in fitness and self-discipline helped to prepare my body for the incredible hardships of the war years. Sadly, not all the Bato gymnasts were so fortunate. When the war was over, three-quarters of our members had perished.

After occupation, my very patriotic mother decided we must try to resist as much as possible, but that was easier said than done. The fact that we were Jewish made it all even more difficult as, immediately after capitulation, decree after decree forced restriction after restriction upon us.

Going to the movies, riding in trams or on bicycles, driving in cars, all were prohibited to us. We were forced to leave our clubs and our friends, as Jews and Christians were not allowed to associate with each other—all this was part of the Nazi plan to isolate the Jewish people from the general population. Life grew more and more perilous every day.

The Nazis tried to win over the Dutch population to their side but they failed. The heroic efforts of the underground movements meant there was never as much as a chance that they would succeed. When their anti–Jewish propaganda didn't have its desired effect, the Nazis showed their real face and the firing squad was almost constantly at work.

I was only seventeen, but I had already met my future husband, Herman Lissing, who had just become involved in the underground Resistance. I can still remember all of us sitting around the table one afternoon, waiting for him to return home after monitoring the news from England. His face was grim when he arrived. Finally he told us about the English radio broadcast. Apparently all the Jews who had been deported to Germany were almost certain to have been gassed or otherwise murdered.

What were we to do? Where could we go?

We did not know, and could see no way out. The underground organisations did as much as they could, but it was still impossible to keep every Jew safe in hiding. The dreaded *Grüne Polizei* (Green Police), an especially brutal Nazi force, carried out constant raids. Not only were the people in hiding shot or deported, but those who had assisted them suffered the same fate.

Mother was the only one of us who did not show any fear. She often said, 'All we can do is to pretend not to care. I would much rather be dead than show them our fear.'

We had to keep her away from the open windows whenever the Nazis marched in the streets, singing about how they would kill everybody who was against *das Reich*. Whenever she had got the chance, she would call out, 'Fatherland traitors and murderers!'

We had to plead with her to think of the rest of the family, as we could all have been shot on the spot, which would have gained nothing. We told her, 'We should only want to live for the liberation and see them go down the gutter.' This usually calmed her down, but to this day I am convinced she would gladly have been shot if only she could have given them 'a piece of her mind'.

It wasn't long before a notice was issued that we had to wear the yellow Star of David, and the first deportations began. There was terrible panic everywhere. Mothers saw their children being taken away, and children were forced to watch their parents being arrested at gunpoint.

Herman wasn't going to wait to be shot or deported. He decided we had better get married at once and then, with the help of the agents of the underground, we would escape to England by travelling along the Belgian, French and Spanish borders and so be able to fight against Nazi Germany.

We applied for our marriage licence at the Registry Office. Under the new Nazi rules, however, a licence could not be issued until a certain number of Jewish couples had applied. Of course, a synagogue wedding was impossible, and Jews were not allowed to marry at the Registry Office. But a former theatre was being used as

This is the last picture taken of us and our parents, on our wedding day. Herman and I were the only survivors—everyone else was killed in Auschwitz.

a Jewish party place, and Jewish civil weddings were performed there.

Four weeks later, we received notice that our marriage could probably take place on the 1st of April, 1942. By the 31st of March, we still had not been told that our wedding could proceed.

Even on the day of our wedding, we were not sure if we would get married, as the Nazis often raided places where they suspected Jews were gathering together. We had to walk the whole way to the

Our wedding day, 1st April 1942. My elegant shoes are actually made of wood. My mother made my beautiful fawn suit and insisted that, war or no war, I had to wear gloves!

theatre, as no form of transport was available for us, and when we arrived, we were astonished to see the place filled with people. There were 25 couples waiting to get married! We were seated in rows in the theatre, some couples by themselves, others accompanied by family.

A civil servant acted as celebrant. He stood on stage, and called out the names of each couple to be wed. Thus we were all married in a mass ceremony.

When we got home, my mother had prepared a lovely lunch for all of us. Although food was scarce, everyone had brought what they could—fresh fish, salads and home-made cake—and we tried to act as if it was a real wedding day. This would be the last time that our whole family was together, and I am forever grateful that we shared that day with all those we loved. Soon afterwards, the first members of our family were deported.

During the war years we lost all our possessions, including our treasured photographs. However, Herman had an aunt by marriage who was not Jewish, and she was able to keep copies of some of our most cherished photographs of our family and our wedding day.

Over the years, Herman and I often talked about our wedding day with a lot of sadness, because of the ridiculous regulations that were imposed upon us.

After the war we met a couple who had been married in the same ceremony. So few people had survived, and it was unusual for both members of a couple to escape with their lives

Life under the Nazis became ever more difficult. Everyone had to carry an identity card, and Jews had a large J inserted on the front page next to the photograph. For those people conscripted to work for the *Wehrmacht* (the German Army), the Nazis placed a *sperre*, or stamp, on their cards, indicating the trade or profession of the bearer. This stamp lulled these people into believing that they were safe from deportation. Then, without warning, the Nazis would declare that the *sperre* of one particular trade, for example workers in a clothing factory, was invalid, and everyone with that particular *sperre* on their card was deported.

Jews were not allowed to leave their homes between eight in the evening and six in the morning. During those hours the Nazi police would break down their victims' doors, and force them into trucks, driving them to the Westerbork transit concentration camp, before deporting them to the gas chambers in Poland and Germany.

The homes of people deported to their deaths were sealed up by the SS. Just a few days later their furniture and belongings, the things people worked for many years to attain, were loaded into trucks and sent to Germany. The firm in charge of this operation was called Puls, and I will never forget that name. Those robbers profited from the torture and death of innocent fellow–citizens. A vile crime.

Herman and I waited, delaying our escape attempt, because I could not bear to leave my family. Then one morning, my elder brother, Maurits, came to our apartment. When I saw his face I knew what had happened. The Nazis had come the night before and had taken my parents and brothers. Because Maurits worked in the diamond trade, and that *sperre* was still valid, he was released.

When the Nazis came to arrest my parents and brothers, they were given only a few minutes to collect some personal belongings to take with them. It was the 10th of November, 1942, my father's 46th birthday. The police kept telling them, 'Hurry up, we don't have time.' Mother slowly turned, faced their tormentors and said she was not afraid to die. She would not change places with them, as they would never ever in their lives find peace with so much blood on their hands.

What affected us most was that while they were standing in the truck, our little brother, Louis, who had acted as though he did not care, pressed close to Maurits and whispered, 'Please don't tell Mummy, but I'm so scared. I don't think they will let us live.'

I can still say that this, despite everything that would happen to me later, was the worst moment of my life. I instantly knew that I would never see my dear family again.

When Maurits was released he was inconsolable, because he had been separated from the rest of the family. Following the usual Nazi procedure, my parents' home was sealed, but Maurits was given a permit to enter under supervision and collect some of his belongings, but nothing else could be touched. Personal possessions like furniture, clothing and photographs all had to be left behind, all of it lost forever. We were allowed to accompany Maurits.

In the kitchen, the food was still on the stove. On the sideboard was a home-made birthday cake for my father. The tears streamed down my face. All I could say was, 'Now I have lost my mother.'

If I had not been so young, I think the shock would have killed me, as I was sure that my life had ended.

The whole of my mother's family would be deported to Poland. In all, five of her brothers and sisters, with their children, were captured at gunpoint. Grandfather was 67 years old in 1942 and was one of the first to be taken. Most of my father's family would suffer the same fate.

The last picture taken of Maurits, the one on his ID card. He was 21. Maurits died in Flossenberg concentration camp in March 1945, only weeks before liberation.

My brother Maurits came to live with us, but after two months the Nazis came and took him away. Now Herman and I were completely alone.

Herman then received notice that he had to register himself with the authorities, as must all former Dutch Air Force officers, so we decided we could not wait any longer. With the help of the underground, we set out for the Belgian border.

I knew our escape would be a dangerous journey, but nothing could keep us from taking this risk. The only alternative we had was to wait until the Nazi police came to the house to arrest us and we knew what that would mean. So we chose to take the risk of being on the run and the chance that we would make it into a free country, thus escaping the Nazi plan for our destruction.

When the opportunity arose for us to set our plan in motion, we had to go ahead. The fact that by now all our loved ones had been taken away gave us the incentive to at least try to stay out of the Nazis' clutches. From the first days of the German invasion, this had been our inner urge, to survive the onslaught and to report what really took place while Holland was under the heel of the Nazi machine of destruction. Herman had been told by the Resistance that he could register himself, as all his Air Force friends were required to do, be interned in a German P.O.W. camp and perhaps survive the war. However, he found out that I would still be moved to a concentration camp in Poland and he felt that the risk was too great.

My mother came from a very musical family. Uncle Sal is playing the accordion, Aunt Rachel the ukulele and Uncle Karl the saxophone. Oma is playing the oboe. The brothers Olevsky, on either side of Oma, were famous German Kapellmeistern *who had fled Germany. They were just two of the many refugees sheltered by my grandparents.*

My father, Jacob, with his first-born, Maurits, at three months of age.

My mother's eldest sister, Anna, with her daughters Nini and Chellie and husband Zak.

My cousins, Shelley and Clare Ereira, Both killed in Auschwitz in 1943

My cousins, Elizabeth, Claire, Appie and Louis Cardozo, who were all killed in May of 1943—gassed in Sobibor extermination camp.

Rachel and Salo (Sal) Lopez Cardozo. Sal was killed in Auschwitz in 1942 and Rachel was gassed in Sobibor extermination camp with her children.

Uncle Karl, the joker of the family, horsing around with Uncle Sal. Both Karl and Sal were killed in Auschwitz.

Grandmother died in Amsterdam in 1939 just before the outbreak of war and grandfather died in September 1942 in Auschwitz, aged 67.

Bato Club outing. Betty aged 14 is fourth from the left. Shelley is second from the left and Nini, standing, is sixth from the left.

Left: Betty, practising gymnastics on the beach, for the Bato Club.

Below: Betty, Olympic Day, November 1937.

CHAPTER TWO

INTO HIDING

Before we could attempt to cross the border into Belgium, we had to go into hiding. An underground agent by the name of Jo Panke had arranged for us to get false identity papers without the compulsory J stamped on the front page.

Getting these papers was so nerve-racking that even to this day I do not know how we survived. Jo Panke had given us one hour to pack a small suitcase and leave the house. He told us to take off the Star of David we had to wear, and meet him in front of a certain building in a well-known city street. There was no time in which to reflect on the sadness I felt in leaving our home, with all the memories it held of such a close and loving family unit. That very evening, the Gestapo arrived to send us to the death camps. At this crucial time, we were one step ahead of them.

When we arrived, Jo gave us a letter and ordered us to go into a building. The letter was to be handed to a man whose name I have now forgotten. As we approached the building's entrance, Herman and I almost froze to the spot. The Nazi swastika was draped across the entrance, over which the words COMMAND POST were prominently displayed.

It was too late to turn back.

We looked at each other, convinced that we had been denounced or fallen into a trap, but outwardly we remained calm as we handed our letter to the doorman.

Without a word he took us to a desk where an officer in a Nazi uniform was seated. Speaking in Dutch, he told us to sit down, and asked me for my identity card. He asked me to follow him into a side room where he took a photograph of me. He was silent until he had finished, when he said, 'Go back to the desk. I will be there soon.'

When I rejoined Herman, he looked at me, his eyes asking, 'What happened out there?' There was no way I could reply.

It is impossible to describe how I felt while we were waiting. My thoughts were whirling round and round. I kept telling myself, 'Steady. Keep focused. Be calm. Everything depends on that.'

When the officer returned, he asked Herman for his identity card. Herman was very blonde, not at all the Nazi idea of a Jewish type. No new photograph of him was necessary.

After what seemed like hours, I was given an entirely new identity card. I was no longer Betty Lissing, née Wynschenk, I was now Annie Keiser.

Herman had his original identity card returned to him, but the J beside his picture had been very skilfully removed. He was still Herman Lissing, but he was no longer a Jew.

The officer stood up and ushered us out.

When we walked out of the building, we saw Jo waiting for us across the street. We were still stunned by our experience at the Gestapo office, but Jo explained that the officer who had given us new identity cards was a Resistance worker.

Jo handed us an address in the western part of Amsterdam. Herman knew the name of the man, as he was an employee at his former workplace. Jo then told us to take the tram to the home of Herman and Margeret Jukkers. This was also risky, as we had not been able to use public transport for the last couple of years. We boarded the tram and someone said, 'Hello Herman, where are you off to?' This man, whom Herman had known for a number of years, did not appear to think it odd to see him, and made no allusion to the fact that Herman was Jewish. Perhaps he just pretended to forget. Nevertheless, we got off the tram a short distance from the Jukkers home just to be on the safe side, and walked the rest of the way.

When we arrived we were greeted with open arms. These simple people were putting their lives on the line by putting us up. If found out, they would be shot. We had to wait there for about three weeks, until our passage to Belgium was arranged in conjunction with the Belgian resistance group *La Brigade Blanche* (The White Brigade).

Those three weeks were extremely hazardous. The Jukkers had told their neighbours that we were cousins from another part of the country, but suspicions were aroused. Local people wanted to know more, including exactly which town we had come from. We could not afford to be caught out in any contradictions, so Herman and I went through many rehearsals with the Jukkers, to make sure our stories matched.

One morning when I was alone in the house, there was a knock at the door.

I opened it and there stood a big police officer, not an ordinary policeman but a uniformed District Inspector.

My heart was beating fast as I asked, 'What can I do for you?'

He said, 'The people next door have put in a complaint. Some of the rabbits they kept in cages have disappeared. We are searching surrounding homes.'

I pretended to be amused and said, 'Go right ahead and look over the place,' —but inside I was really terrified. What if our protectors or Herman returned home and lost their cool at the sight of the policeman?

The Inspector looked around and said, 'Thank you. They are certainly not here, unless you have eaten them already.'

During the whole time in that village we were in constant fear of the locals and their suspicions. Would they go to the police, and denounce us and the Jukkers to the Nazis? All our lives were on the line.

Food was very scarce but the Jukkers shared whatever they could buy with us.

Every day that we could extend our freedom was of the utmost importance, and after the war we discovered just how vital that extra time was for us. Practically none of the prisoners sent to Auschwitz in the early transports survived.

We were given the go-ahead to leave Holland on Whitsunday, 1943. It was assumed that we would be less conspicuous if we travelled on a holiday weekend. When we said goodbye to the Jukkers family we were both in tears.

The plan was for us to take the train to the village of Lage-Mierde in the province of Brabant, on the Belgian border, where the Panke family had a farm. Jo would be waiting for us with bicycles at the station. From there it would take about half an hour to reach the farm.

Herman and I entered the central station in the heart of Amsterdam early on the Saturday morning of the holiday weekend. No sooner had we joined the queue for tickets, however, than the Gestapo, their guns drawn, raided the station and blocked all entrances and exits. Panic broke out, fuelled by the usual threats and shouting by the SS officers. People were made to stand in line with their identity cards ready for inspection.

Herman and I somehow remained in control of our panic. We tried to behave like holiday-makers, looking almost nonchalant as, one by one, the crowd filed past the police. Then it was my turn. The SS officer looked at me, held up my identity card, and nodded to me to proceed. Herman was next, and this was the real test as his card had been tampered with at Gestapo headquarters. The officer took his card, held it up to the light, looked at him, looked at the card again, and then nodded him on.

We ran to the waiting train, shaking like leaves, but with smiles on our faces.

The train was packed with German soldiers, who travelled all over Holland. We blocked out all fear, because one wrong move on our part would give us away. It took about three hours to arrive at our destination, where Jo was waiting for us as promised, with the bicycles.

The Pankes welcomed us with kindness and a good meal. We would have to wait three days at the farm for Guus Willemse, a gendarme with the Belgian police. Guus was a member of the Brigade Blanche, who would provide us with false Belgian papers and guide us over the border into Belgium.

Lage-Mierde is close to the Belgian border. Its population,

mostly farmers, were staunch Catholics, part of a close–knit community, where everyone knew everyone else. Being Whitsunday, church services were well attended. Jo told us we should go to church with his family, so as not to appear different. This was a new experience for us, but no one seemed suspicious, as we mingled with the congregation. I don't know if the villagers knew why we were there. They did not ask any questions. But when we left Lage–Mierde three days later, most of the people came out and waved us off saying, 'God bless you'.

It was late in the afternoon when we met Guus, and we prepared to cross the border. Herman, Jo and Guus were each riding a bicycle. I rode on the luggage seat of Jo's bicycle. Of course we could not risk a light, so we made our way in darkness. No one spoke.

The woods were so dense that we often had to get off our bicycles and walk. But open spaces were dangerous. The Germans had guards with dogs all over the place, as well as powerful searchlights. To remain unseen, we often had to crawl on our bellies, dragging the bicycles after us. If they sighted anyone in the woods, the Germans would shoot first without bothering to ask questions.

Our destination was the border village of Weelde in Belgium, where Guus lived with his parents. It was only about 30 kilometres from the Panke farm, but getting there seemed to be an endless trek. Rain was pelting into our faces. Twigs and branches from the trees cut and scratched us, but we hardly noticed, we were concentrating so intensely on getting across the border. We could see the searchlights and hear voices in the distance, but the heavy rain and the darkness actually worked in our favour, hiding us from view.

Suddenly we were beyond the trees and in an open paddock. The ground was very muddy so we had to walk slowly beside our bicycles. After what seemed to be hours, we saw a farm with lights shining from the windows. It was an immense relief to hear Guus say, 'Yes, that is our house. We have made it.'

Again we were received with kindness and a meal. After a hot bath, we collapsed, exhausted, in the barn. Early the next morning, after a good breakfast, we thanked the Willemse family for their kindness and set out on our bicycles, pretending to be holiday-makers enjoying a ride in the country.

There was a hotel in the village of Weelde, where we had to wait for our Belgian identity cards, without which it would be impossible to travel through Belgium. The lounge of the hotel was filled with German soldiers waiting to board a train.

There were also some locals drinking beer, who stared at us curiously as not many strangers came to this hotel. Herman noticed the piano, and asked the owner if he could play it, saying he was a musician on his way to an engagement in Brussels. Before long, everyone was singing along with the music. I stared at Herman in amazement, and he winked at me. He later told me it was better to act brazenly and carry on.

When Jo Panke finally appeared in the hotel lounge with the false papers hidden in his pocket, he could not believe his eyes and ears. He had landed in the middle of a sing-along. I was really shaking inwardly, but Herman seemed totally at ease, and smiled when the soldiers applauded.

After dinner, Jo gave us our passports. We were now Maria and Herman Machielse, from Lembekke in Belgium. Guus and Jo took us to the station, settled us in a compartment and said goodbye. We had a contact address in Brussels, but it was to be used only in an emergency. So Herman and I were on our own, on our way to an unknown destination. Fortunately we both spoke the local Flemish dialect, because without that, we could not hope to remain inconspicuous. Surely we would have more chance of remaining anonymous in a big city like Brussels.

However, when we arrived we discovered that our contact man had been arrested, so we had to stay in Brussels longer than we had hoped. We had very little money, but Herman found work in a bar playing the piano. I did not go out any more than strictly necessary. For Herman it was easier. Musicians, working late hours, were given special passes which allowed them to be out after curfew. Herman spoke French as well as English and German, so he started working for the Belgian underground by carrying messages all over the city.

We felt a great sense of relief to be in Brussels, after life in occupied Holland. Although Belgium of course was also occupied, there did not seem to be the same sense of terror in the streets, and there was more food available in the shops. The fact that we were anonymous in our new surroundings added to our new sense of security. If our journey to Spain for some reason could not go ahead, perhaps we would be safe here.

We began to establish a daily routine, although always on the alert for the unexpected. Herman continued his work with the Resistance, until one afternoon he was arrested by the German police, who had followed him all day. When I received word of his arrest, the Resistance immediately advised me to leave the house where we were renting our room, and keep on the move till further notice, in case Herman was forced to reveal where I was living. I had to keep out of easy reach of the Nazis.

I moved from room to room and one night slept on a park bench, until at last I received the 'all clear' from our contact. Herman had been moved to the transit camp of Malines, before being deported to Poland.

I went back to the boarding house where we had been staying. Jo Panke came to see me and gave me some money. Shortly after, though, Jo himself was arrested. This was another crisis. It was very difficult to be alone in a new country, and I badly needed support. To be alone, with no means of earning a living, was a frightening prospect. It was too dangerous for me to try to get work without revealing who I was. I lived only one day at a time, and dared not even contemplate the future.

In an attempt to persuade Jews in the occupied countries that their affairs would be taken care of, the Nazis set up special Jewish Councils. Their chief function was to pacify Jews who were to be deported, but with their help, I was able to send Herman some food parcels and some letters.

Herman was arrested on the 10th of August, 1943. He was kept at Malines Transit Camp until he was deported to Auschwitz in

September, 1943. He had always told me that he would try to escape if he was ever caught and deported. I hoped and prayed that he would succeed.

(After liberation Herman told me he had tried to escape, but the wagons in his transport were too heavily guarded. This was because the transport before had been ambushed by the Belgian Resistance. People broke out while the trains were still travelling through Belgium. Most of the escapees were shot, but a few managed to stay in hiding.)

I struggled on alone for about six weeks. Fortunately, I spoke a little French and managed to buy food at the local shops. Early one morning, on the 25th of September, 1943, I heard loud voices in the house, and a lot of shouting. I knew I was in trouble. I stayed hidden in my room until suddenly the door was pushed open and two Gestapo officers armed with revolvers burst into the room and demanded my identity papers.

All the occupants of the house were arrested, and we were taken to the Gestapo prison in Avenue Louise. This prison had a gruesome reputation, and was very much feared because it was said that prisoners were brutally beaten and tortured until they confessed why they were in hiding; whether they were Jews or political opponents of the Nazis.

At the prison I was interrogated by two SS officers. They had rung Lembekke to verify my identity and of course there was no evidence of a Maria Machielse. They knew I was Jewish. They shouted and threatened me, but I did not say a word.

Suddenly one of the officers turned to me, lowered his voice and said, 'You are beautiful, and you don't have to be deported, if you will reveal the names of others in hiding.'

I remained silent.

'In that case, we have no choice but to deport you.'

From Avenue Louise I was taken to St Gilles prison. The cell I was taken to was like an underground bunker. I was one of its first occupants, as a group of prisoners had just been transferred to Malines, the transit camp from which all transports left for Poland.

There were no facilities in the bunker, not even a bench to lie on, and we had to sit huddled together on the floor. On the second day, a family of three was brought in, a grandmother, daughter and child. They had been in hiding, but had been denounced.

Every hour, an SS officer would come into our cell and bark obscenities at his hapless prisoners. One time, he looked at the grandmother, who was wearing a beautiful fur coat. Suddenly, he yelled at her.

'Spread that coat on the floor and let the Dutch woman lie down on it!'

I said, 'Oh no, I don't want to,' but the grandmother winked at me, and said, 'Certainly, sir.'

As soon as the guard had left I jumped up and gave her back her coat. She said, 'When he comes back, just do what he says and don't protest. He could shoot us all.'

Her little red-haired granddaughter, who must have been about nine years old, was watching us with big, solemn eyes.

The Jewish Council arranged food supplies for us, but most of us could not eat, as we were so apprehensive about what lay ahead of us.

After three days I was put on a truck with other prisoners and taken to Malines transit camp, where I remained for about three months.

Malines was an old military barracks, and the guards were Flemish fascists and German police. Prisoners were confined there until there were sufficient numbers to make up a transport to Poland.

Life in Malines was bearable, as the Brussels Jewish Council was allowed to supply the prisoners with food but this was another psychological ploy of the Nazis. The fact that the Jewish Council was allowed to function lulled free members of the community into a false sense of security. Then, very swiftly and without warning, yet another building would be seized and all its occupants arrested and deported.

At Malines men, women and children lived and slept on wooden boards in long dormitories. There were daily inspections by the guards, and we lived in constant dread that at any moment we would be deported.

Eventually, one morning we were ordered to line up with the little clothing that we had with us. We were led out of the camp, under police guard, to a ramp where cattle trucks were waiting. Men, women, children, the sick and the frail, all were pushed and forced into the trucks, 80 persons to a wagon. There was no food or water and the only facility was a bucket in a corner. When the doors were closed it was pitch–dark inside.

Packed into the wagon was a cross–section of the general community. There were lawyers, university professors, famous musicians and everyday decent workers with their children. Hitler made no distinction between us – every person in those cattle cars was marked for extermination.

If one had any doubt before entering the wagon that this was a journey to death, the horror of that ride left no doubt about its outcome. Perhaps the worst part was the suffering of the children and their mothers. Children were crying for food, and mothers had nothing to give them. Such vile treatment made us feel doomed. In despair we tried to comfort each other, especially the crying children.

I particularly remember the little redheaded girl from the holding cell. I am sure she must have felt the end was near, because she could not speak and would not listen when I tried to comfort her. With her eyes wide open she cried and cried all the time.

By the last day of the journey, most people were resigned to their fate. They expected the worst to happen, and it did.

CHAPTER THREE

AUSCHWITZ-BIRKENAU

After three days of no water, food, light or fresh air, the train pulled into a siding at Auschwitz–Birkenau.

The doors opened and the guards began shouting at us to get out onto the ramp. As we stumbled out of the train we were told to leave our personal belongings beind, as they would be brought into the camps by the prison guards. Of course, we never saw our things again.

There were SS officers everywhere, with whips and dogs at their sides, shouting, 'Men to the left, women to the right.'

At the end of the ramp were army trucks with the Red Cross painted on them. A disembodied voice screamed at us over the loudspeaker that mothers and children had to go on the trucks, as well as anyone who was old or tired.

I had travelled from the Malines with a Dutch family. The father had to leave his wife and 17–year–old daughter, and stand with the other men on the left side of the platform.

The women had to file past a group of SS officers, one of whom would become familiar to almost every woman in the camp – Dr Mengele. (His infamy has been well documented, but as I was never chosen for medical experiments, I had no personal contact with him.)

As the Dutch mother filed past, one of the officers told her to go on the truck. Her beautiful daughter asked to go with her, and the officer said 'Yes'. I wanted to stay with my friends, so I asked if I could go with them.

In answer, the officer raised his whip and struck me across the head, before pushing me away from them.

I also saw the little red–haired girl, together with her mother and grandmother, walking towards the truck. As the trucks moved off, I was marched away with 80 other young women and girls.

After ten minutes we entered Auschwitz–Birkenau *Frauenlaager* (Women's Camp). Over the entrance, in large letters, was a sign which proclaimed that *Arbeit Macht Frei* (Work makes free). We were marched into a so–called bathroom, where the prison guards ordered us to take off all our clothes. We also had to hand over our wedding rings and anything else the Belgian prison officials had overlooked. Our hair was shaved off, our arms tattooed with a number and then we were handed the filthiest, bloodstained, bug–ridden prison clothes imaginable. No underwear or stockings were provided because, as the guards callously told us, we would have no need for them, as none of us would come out of the camp alive. We would certainly be gassed or otherwise murdered.

When I asked one of the women guards if I would see my friends who had been put on the trucks again, she told me point blank that they were just then being gassed and burned. Through a little window in the bathroom, she showed me the flames and fumes coming out of the crematorium.

I stared at her, thinking that she must have gone mad, but she was giving me the facts. None of us would survive. Hundreds of thousands of prisoners, from all the German–occupied countries, had been gassed or murdered already.

'Don't think,' she said, 'you will come out because you have been saved on arrival. If you don't go immediately to the gas chamber in the camp, it's even worse. There is no water, no food. There is typhoid and cholera, and under camp conditions you will not be able to survive anyway.'

I asked her about all the Dutch people who had been deported already. They had died quickest, she said. I later realised that because they had never endured any hardships, they were least of all prepared for the horrors of the camps. So it was true. My mother, father, brothers, relatives and friends – they were all dead. That meant Herman must have died, too.

'Dear God,' I prayed, 'I need more courage, because I cannot take it. I would rather die now than go through it all with no will to live.'

I would be unable to speak, or to utter any sound, for three days.

We were kept in the bathroom for 24 hours, then we were marched through the snow-covered camp to the quarantine block.

The stench of burning bodies was everywhere.

There was nothing in the hut but wooden boards on which to sleep, six of us to one board, with one filthy, bug-ridden blanket between us. We could not stretch out but had to sleep crouched like animals, as the boards measured only about 6 feet by 2 feet.

'I have landed in Dante's Inferno,' I remember thinking. 'It really exists and this is the place.'

The next morning our *Kapos* (warders) whipped us awake. The *Kapos* were also prisoners but, because they could control large groups of other prisoners, mainly through their own brutality, they were in a better position than the rest of us. It was the *Kapos* who distributed food to each prisoner.

Shivering with fright, cold and hunger, we stood in line outside. The temperature must have been well below zero. Dressed only in our rags we were soon covered in snow. After what seemed to be all day (but was only about three hours) we were again marched to the bathroom, as the doctor wanted to 'look us over'.

That was a laugh. Here we were, stumbling over dead and dying bodies, consisting of nothing but skin and bone, and the doctor wanted to look us over!

When we got to the bathroom, we could hear terrible screams and cries coming from prisoners who were trying to resist going into the bathroom.

We soon found out why they were so terrified.

We had to undress again and pass in single file before the so-called 'doctors', who were, of course, SS officers, who stood with pencil and paper in hand. Every so often they would take down the number on a victim's arm. We were then ordered to get dressed and march back to our block, where we were locked in.

That night we were each given a small wooden bowl, or *schutsel*, containing a meagre portion of watery soup. After five days of no food or water, however, it tasted very good. That bowl would become our most important possession. If it was lost or stolen it would not be replaced, and without their *schutsel*, no one would receive any liquid food.

That evening the doors of the hut burst open and a number of SS officers entered, with the ominous lists in their hands. The hut *Kapo* was called to the entrance and those prisoners who had had their numbers taken earlier were called out. Some of the women began to panic and screams broke out. The condemned women tried to hide, but there was nowhere for them to go. They were pushed into open carts at gunpoint. I have never forgotten the sight of these struggling young girls desperately trying to hang on to the doorposts of the huts.

Their pitiful cries for help slowly died away as they were driven to the gas chambers.

At first I was tempted to give in to the wish to die rather than struggle to hang on under these conditions, but my inner drive for survival was so strong that I could not give up. I later realised that even to remain alive in Auschwitz was a form of resistance.

I remember a special transport of 600 young, healthy Dutch girls (my sister–in–law among them) arriving at the camp. They were immediately put to work without 'selection'. When they became aware of the horrors of Auschwitz, however, they lost the will to live and within weeks there were only eight of them still alive. They just gave up, welcoming death as a way out of their misery.

For the next four weeks, we were made to carry bricks from one end of the camp to the other, for no other reason but to keep us busy. Then we were again marched to the dreaded bathroom, and had to pass again in single file again before our tormentors. One of them pulled me out of the line, and wrote down my number. A few of the other women suffered the same fate.

Was this the end?

I felt numb with shock, but at the same time I tried to remain alert to what was happening around me. The girls whose numbers had been taken clung together, expecting the worst. Although I was terrified, the feeling that I would survive came flooding over me. I prayed fervently to myself, 'Don't let this be the end. I need to carry on.'

I held myself still, waiting.

CHAPTER FOUR

THE UNION BARRACKS

I thought that my time had come. Most of the women with whom I had marched into Auschwitz had died already. Selection could happen at any moment, and we knew it meant certain death. But I had been chosen to work in the munitions factory, the Union Kommando. I was put on the night shift, from seven in the evening to seven in the morning, seven days a week.

Together with the other women who had been selected, I was marched to the entrance of the union barracks, where we were met by our new *Kapo*, who said, 'These are your living and sleeping quarters.'

The hut was bleak, dark and crudely assembled. There were tiers of three wooden boards, one on top of the other and about two metres wide. Six to eight women had to sleep on one board, with one filthy blanket between them.

Our *Kapo*'s name was Paula. She was Polish, but had lived all her life in Paris.

'Do as you are told and don't make any problems,' she told us. 'We are all trying to survive. Conditions are atrocious, and there are many selections. Every time new transports arrive, the SS call for a selection of the women who are getting weaker, and replace them with stronger new arrivals.'

Paula's own face was etched with suffering. She had seen so many women perish, women who had been relatively healthy when they had arrived just weeks before. I think she was truly heartbroken, but she could do nothing to help any one. Her life was in just as much peril as that of any other prisoner. I do not know if she survived the hell of Auschwitz. So few did.

Food was less than meagre. Our daily ration was a small piece of mouldy bread and a mug of what was called 'coffee', but in reality was just brown water. There was no way to obtain extra water and other fluids were impossible to find. We were always icy cold and desperately thirsty. We died like flies on a wall.

We knew when our fellow prisoners were doomed. They lost their spirit and walked around like the living dead. We called them *Musselmanner* (walking skeletons) and mercifully they died quickly.

Every morning, we had to remove dead bodies from the barracks. They were picked up by the crematorium squad and taken away for burning. The terrible stench of burning bodies was ever present in the camp.

Despair and horror were all around us. Adding to the nightmare was the arrival of new transports, packed with people who shortly would be gassed to death. Frightened and confused, but still trusting in the lies of their betrayers, they would be met by SS officers who with one hand would gently stroke the heads of the savage dogs at their side and with the other lead little girls still hugging their dolls into the gas chamber.

Even to this day I do not know how I came through those hours, days and months. I do know that I blocked out any emotion. I never dared to think about my home life and the free world, for I knew that if I did, I would not be able to endure my present surroundings. And yet I always had an inner feeling that I would survive. What it was that gave me that feeling I don't know, as no one was ever closer to death than those in Auschwitz's destruction camp.

I did not permit myself to pray formally for the strength to survive this ordeal, but now, when I look back, I can identify those periods when I was overcome by utter despair. At times when there seemed no way out of the horrors around me, I was overtaken by a complete inner stillness. When that happened, I always lost my voice. All I know is that at these times there was a 'presence' around me that helped me carry on, a protective cocoon, a kind of mental hiding place. When 'selections' took place, my life was in immediate danger. Then I relied on that inner feeling of support that took over when I was totally still.

Rebecca, my cousin from Brussels, visited Australia only once in 1976. This picture of the two 'Betties' was taken in front of my house. It is not surprising we did not recognise each other sooner in the Union Barracks of Auschwitz, since our last meeting had been five years previously, and she always lived in Belgium. Besides, our heads were shaved, our faces were drawn and hollow, and we were wearing filthy prison clothes.

CHAPTER FIVE

THE UNION MUNITIONS FACTORY

At least working inside in the Union Munitions Factory was better than having to work outside in the freezing snow. Everyone who worked the night shift received an extra bowl of soup at midnight. These extra rations meant the difference between life and death.

The work was not only hard but hazardous, as we were watched continually by SS officers and prison guards. If someone was seen to stop work for a moment, or if faulty parts were found mixed up with the good ones, it was considered sabotage, and vicious punishments would result, not just for the individual, but for all the workers on that particular table.

I remember one such incident when all the women working on one table were severely punished for sabotage. We were all forced to watch as camp commandant Hössler, who appeared demented from rage, screamed threats of imminent death while he flogged his victims mercilessly. The entire work detail was in shock, but we could do nothing to help these women. When they were taken away, all bleeding badly, we assumed that they would be gassed. Two days later, however, they were all returned to the block. This was the madness of the Nazi culture.

Punishments were never inflicted during work periods, always in meal breaks. The prison guards also seemed to find it amusing to make us kneel on the concrete floor holding our stools above our heads, or force us to do floor gymnastics. I kept telling myself, 'Be calm, they want you to collapse and lose control,' but to remain constantly mentally alert demanded enormous will power.

I remember all the faces and horrors of Auschwitz, but especially four young women who were hanged in front of all the slave labourers of the Union Munitions Factory, on the 6th of January, 1945. A few months previously, these four young women had smuggled gunpowder from the munitions room to the men working in one of the camp crematoria. These men were responsible for the cremation of the gassed bodies of the prisoners and were known as the *Sonder Kommando*.

These *Sonder Kommando* were continually being replaced by new arrivals, as no one who worked in the crematoria was allowed to live for more than a few months. They, in their turn, were also gassed.

In October, 1944, one crematorium, (I think it was No. 4) was blown up with the smuggled dynamite and put out of action. The *Sonder Kommando* rose up in revolt, an uprising which the Nazis crushed by putting everyone who worked at the crematoria to death.

The accused young women were all tortured and sentenced to hang – two in front of the day shift, two in front of the night shift. These four young girls were incredibly brave. I shall never forget one of them who, just before the noose was placed around her neck, lifted her head up high and called out, 'Wake up, all of you, wake up!'

This picture stayed with me for years, and I am convinced that she saw beyond the horror of that moment and looked into infinity, where she could not be touched by her tormentors.

The young sister of one of the accused had to endure the agonising horror of her beloved companion's hanging. The two sisters were very close and had both struggled so much to survive. I was told that the surviving girl lost all will to go on, but her friends in the camp refused to let her go, and carried her through this added ordeal. In the end, she survived. After liberation she married and now lives in Canada.

Some years ago, a monument to the four murdered girls was unveiled in Israel. They paid with their lives for their heroic deeds, but they will never be forgotten by the remaining Union Munitions Factory survivors.

I vowed, if the impossible ever came about and the war came to an end, I would return to that place as a free person, and sink to my knees and pay homage to every soul who perished by the hands of the Nazis, here on this forsaken spot.

I have never gone back since liberation, but I travel there often in my meditations, to unite with those blessed souls who did not come home.

There is an unbreakable bond between the survivors of the death camps, a pain which is so deeply embedded in our souls that it cannot be explained to anyone who has not lived through our experiences. Despite this, however, it is amazing that most of us can carry on with our lives and enjoy the blessings of our families and friends. These blessings give us the incentive to live meaningful lives.

Of the 150 women in the union barracks, I thought I was the only Dutch national, so I was surprised when one of the women told me that there was another Dutch woman in the day shift. She knew nothing about this woman, as we were only known by our numbers.

One afternoon a young woman came up to me and asked if I was Dutch. When I answered her in the affirmative, she stared hard at me and asked my name. When I told her she said, 'No, your maiden name.'

'Wynschenk.'

She stared at me and cried, 'You are my cousin. Oh my God, the only friend I had was taken to the gas chamber last week, and now I have found you.'

It is not surprising we did not recognise each other, since our last meeting had been five years previously, and she always lived in Belgium. Besides, our heads were shaved, our faces were drawn and hollow, and we were wearing filthy prison clothes. I doubt if our own mothers could have recognised us.

Rebecca had made it as far as the South of France with her husband, father and mother—my aunt—and her brother and sister-in-law. From there, the men crossed safely into Spain. The next day Rebecca, her mother and sister-in-law left to join them but, after robbing them of their money and jewellery, their guide denounced them to the Gestapo.

Rebecca's mother was gassed on their arrival at Auschwitz and her sister-in-law Maria, who was not Jewish, was sent to the concentration camp at Ravensbruck. (This was a camp mainly for non-Jewish political prisoners from all occupied countries, but it also included German political opponents of the Nazis.) Maria survived.

From the moment we found each other, Rebecca and I tried to keep together as much as possible.

Shortly after starting work at the munitions factory, I fell ill. My body was on fire with a fever, and I felt as though my head would burst. Among the workers at my table was a Greek doctor. He looked across at me and quietly said, 'My child, you have typhus.'

When I next saw Rebecca I told her I was going to the *Revier*, the inmates' hospital, a decision that would mean certain death, but Rebecca coaxed and bullied me and would not let me report sick. With her support I worked my shift in the factory and neither the *Kapos* nor the SS guards ever suspected how ill I was. How I survived that particular ordeal, I still do not know.

And so Rebecca and I supported each other, covered for each other and saved each other's life on many occasions. To this day I can say that neither of us would have survived if we had not found each other. We worked, stood roll call for hours in the bitter cold, saw our fellow-prisoners being gassed, burned, hung and shot, had barely enough to eat and, like everyone else, stole food whenever we could.

Every evening our column of women walked to the munitions factory to begin the night shift. This walk took about 25 minutes. Close by the factory was a railway line, which we crossed by an elevated bridge. Below us in the darkness, the sombre–looking carriages took civilian coal miners home to their families in the next village. I remember looking down, watching the trains making their turn into the distance, and thinking, 'Oh, if I could ever experience the freedom of going home again to a normal life, I would be the most blessed person in the world.' I do not know where this thought came from, as it seemed completely far–fetched – how could I even contemplate such a wish?

Towards the end of 1944, we were returning from work in the factory one morning when we passed a column of prisoners from the men's camp, who were going to work. Whenever I found myself

Sam and Sophia. Sophia died in Auschwitz on the 30th of January 1944.

near such a group, I always called out softly, 'Are there any Dutchmen among you?'

This time, a voice, just above a whisper, answered, 'Yes, I am Dutch.'

When I looked closer, to my disbelief I saw that it was my brother-in-law, Sam Lissing. The next day, our columns passed each other again, and Sam and I managed to whisper briefly to each other.

'I saw Herman a little while ago,' Sam told me, 'but he was very ill and really dying, so do not expect him to return. He was too far gone.'

I thought then that I would never see either Herman or Sam again. For my part, I could not tell Sam that his beautiful young wife, Sophia, had died in Auschwitz on the 30th of January, 1944. That would have made his struggle for survival all the more difficult.

Towards the end of 1944, the behaviour of our SS guards became even more erratic, and we began to dare to believe that the war was not going the way they had planned. The flame of resistance still burned in the camp, and we whispered stories of hope amongst ourselves, but we were all still convinced that we would not be allowed to survive the war. The death toll was enormous. The Russians were advancing rapidly, and the directive from Gestapo headquarters was that no eye-witness should be left alive to testify to the atrocities of the camps. More than ever, our lives were hanging by a thread.

CHAPTER SIX

THE DEATH MARCH

On the night of the 18th of January, 1945, we were suddenly told to line up, as we were being moved to another camp. I had been in Auschwitz for eighteen months.

What we did not know was that the Russians were only a few kilometres from the camp, and the German army was in retreat. Not wanting to leave any live evidence of their atrocities the Nazis decided to take their starved and sick prisoners with them into Germany, and so began another terrible and tragic journey.

We marched through the snow, heavily guarded by SS guards and Wehrmacht soldiers with guns and pistols. Those who could not keep up, and there were many, were shot. We were continually stumbling over dead bodies.

We marched through the snow for 110 kilometres, without food or water.

The second night of that march will never be erased from my mind. As the column of young women ploughed its way through the snow, icy winds howled around us and we could barely breathe. Suddenly we were being attacked by Russian planes. We automatically dropped to the ground and lay face down in the snow, but there was nowhere to hide as we were in an open field. The guards were screaming in panic. We all had to lie in the snow until the air-raid was over. The absolute terror of that episode is indelibly engraved in my innermost being.

When we were again forced to march on, many frozen bodies were left behind.

The whole march took place at gunpoint. The prison guards were just as panic-stricken as we were, and they vented their fear and anger on their defenceless charges. They told us continuously that they would shoot us rather than allow the Russians to liberate us. We knew they meant it and most of us struggled on, driven only by our basic instinct to survive.

Finally we arrived at the siding of a small station called Loslau, in Upper Silesia. Even now, the SS guards were still shooting randomly into the column of defenceless prisoners.

We were loaded onto open trains, with no protection from the snow, and with no food or water. Although many of us had been shot or died of cold during the march, we were still too many for the transports. We were so cramped in the trains that it was impossible to sit down or even stand up without treading on or pushing into someone else.

Fights broke out among the prisoners, most of whom were delirious from thirst. Had it been summer none of us would have survived. We lapped up the life-saving snow like dogs.

Our guards, however, ate their rations and drank their brandy from the flasks that they each had hung around their bodies.

After a day of waiting in the open trucks, we moved off, crisscrossing war-torn Germany. Everywhere we saw only dead bodies, and later we heard that all the camps had been evacuated.

After six days of dumping frozen bodies out of the wagons, we came to Ravensbruck, the camp for women political prisoners near Berlin.

About half of the prisoners had gone mad. As soon as they were released from the trucks they ran wild and were gunned down on the spot.

The conditions at Ravensbruck were just as terrible as those at any other camp. The camp officials did not know what to do with us. The remnants of our pathetic group were hustled into a barrack.

There was still no water, no food and I felt myself going into a decline. We all huddled together on the muddy, frozen ground. The next morning a few large buckets of boiled, unpeeled potatoes were thrown among us, which caused a terrible fight. I must have lost consciousness during that fight, because I came to with a potato clasped in each hand.

That afternoon we were led outside, to find large buckets of water on the parade ground. We threw ourselves face down into the water, everyone fighting desperately to drink. This was the only time I saw tears in the eyes of the German guards. I know from my experiences that thirst is far worse than hunger.

By now, it was the end of January, and Rebecca and I were both in a state of utter despair. Because the camp was so crowded, the only space available for us was in the punishment block. There were no bunks, and we were forced to sleep huddled together on the floor.

We still had to gather for roll call outside in the snow. One day, I found myself standing close to a small hut. I looked through its window and saw three very emaciated, sick young women lying on a bunk. One of them spoke in French to the woman next to me. Her name was Violet Szabo, and she told us that she and her two companions were to be shot the next day.

Which they were.

At the time, her name meant nothing to me. It was only after the war that I learned of her courage – indeed the film made to honour her could not have had a better title than *To Carve her Name with Pride*.

We were all close to death, but that no longer made any impression on us. By now, death was a familiar and close companion. Such was the culture of the Third Reich. It was not life they represented, for wherever the Nazis went, they brought death with them.

We stayed at Ravenbruck for three weeks. Then, on the 11th of February, my 22nd birthday, the remaining members of our transport were again loaded onto trains.

After about twelve hours, we arrived at another camp—Neustadt–Glewe in Mecklenburg. Most of us were in state of collapse. How did we stay alive? I don't know.

Neustadt–Glewe was a small camp and could not cope with the influx of so many sick and starved prisoners. There was hardly any organisation in the camp, and most of the prisoners were confined to the barracks, where no facilities were available. No food or water was distributed and girls were dying all around us.

Only days before our liberation, we were lined up again outside the barracks. We had to file past the SS guards and some of us were given a pink card. We never found out the significance of the pink card.

Rumours spread that we were to be transported to Sweden, which was a neutral country. This did not happen in Neustadt-Glewe, but I later found out that many prisoners from nearby camps reached the river Elbe on the way to Sweden. They were loaded on to barges which were then deliberately scuttled. Most of the prisoners either drowned or were shot in the water, although a very few did escape to Sweden.

Germany was in disarray on all fronts by now. The orders that came through from headquarters were confusing, even to the SS, but this did not change their motivation which, at all times, was to kill the prisoners. No living evidence of their crimes was to be left behind. At some camps they achieved their goal. All the prisoners were slaughtered.

At Neustadt-Glewe, women died from hunger and total exhaustion. When a person is in such a poor condition, the easiest thing is just to slip away, and the temptation to do so is great. For my part, however, I grimly clung to life. By now I was barefoot as my wooden shoes had been lost during the death march, and I could barely move.

More and more planes were roaring overhead. We prayed to be bombed so we could be put out of our misery.

One day, after two months of suffering and despair, the Germans locked us in our hut and for twelve hours we did not hear a sound. I could no longer stand and I was semi-conscious. I remember thinking, 'If I close my eyes, I will die.'

Suddenly we heard a lot of noise. One of the political prisoners looked through the tiny window and recognised the vehicle outside.

'It's a Jeep!'

Then she screamed, 'Americans! They are Americans!'

CHAPTER SEVEN

LIBERATION
2nd of May, 1945

The Americans entered the camp unhindered. All the German guards and SS had fled. Our liberators unlocked all the huts, and found a storeroom filled to the brim with potatoes, carrots and other vegetables, as well as loaves of bread. They could not stay but told us that Russian tanks were coming. The Third Reich, that was going to exist gloriously for a thousand years, was now in tatters and facing certain defeat.

Rebecca kept shaking me and begging me to get up. I remember thinking listlessly, 'What a pity. They have come too late to save me.'

I have no clear recollection of what was happening around me. I was carried outside on a door which someone had found. Some of the women managed to make a fire into which they threw potatoes, and they also made soup. I do remember someone putting hot soup into my mouth.

The Russians arrived that afternoon. They had no idea that there was a small camp hidden in this area. They had no food to give us, but they killed a horse, and told those of us who could still walk to go into the village of Neustadt, go into the houses and take whatever food we could find. Those who went to the village found most of the houses deserted. The occupants had fled in fear from the advancing Russian troops. Surprisingly, the empty homes contained lots of food the owners had left behind. Most of the girls ate all they could hold, but paid dearly for it by becoming very sick afterwards. Some even died. Their starved bodies could not handle the food.

Many of the women brought food back for those of us who had remained in the camp. Some of us managed to survive on what we found to eat, but lots of us died in the early days after liberation as there was no medical help available. I was later told it was fortunate that I had not obtained much food straight after liberation. My body had to adjust slowly to normal nourishment.

After three more weeks in the camp the Russians took those of us from Western Europe over the Elbe into the American zone. From there the Americans slowly started to repatriate survivors to their homelands.

On the 21st of May, riding in a Red Cross army truck, I arrived in Enschede, in Holland.

I remember thinking, 'If I can only reach Holland before I die, I will be happy.' I stubbornly refused to die on German soil. When we crossed the border between Germany and Holland I cried for the first time in two years, when I saw Dutch people standing at the roadside, with little national flags in their hands.

I was taken to an emergency hospital. I weighed only 37 kilos (74 lbs) and was suffering from severe malnutrition, anaemia and gall bladder trouble. I was in a badly depleted state. After three weeks in hospital I still was not able to eat properly. I had lost my reason for existence, because none of my beloved family were left alive. I had been told that Herman had died. I might have survived the ordeal but now I had no reason for living.

It was decided that I should be sent to Castle Eerde in Ommen. The castle belonged to Baron van Palland, who had been interned by the Nazis as a hostage during the occupation of the Netherlands. He had been lucky not to be shot, the fate of so many other hostages. When he returned home, he dedicated himself to helping his surviving countrymen recuperate on his beautiful estate. He converted his castle into a hospital for survivors of concentration camps who needed extra special care.

Castle Eerde was a blessing. There I took my first steps to recovery, even though it was discovered that I was also suffering from tuberculosis. The staff, most of whom had been in the

Resistance, were very kind.

Occupation forces were stationed nearby. When they found out that we patients in the castle hospital were concentration camp survivors, they sent gifts of chocolates and sweets. The Baron came to visit the patients daily, bearing baskets of fresh flowers from the gardens. He usually took time to chat with me, encouraging me to go on with my life. He also invited me to his house on the estate, where I met his wife and daughters.

The tranquillity of the estate was soothing balm to my soul and I often found a great urge to touch the shrubs and flowers growing in the gardens. This had a cleansing effect on me. I had a great need to rid myself of all the horror and ugliness I had lived through. It would be many years, however, before I could automatically accept the beauty of nature as a normal experience.

In order to survive the ordeal of the camps, I had blocked out most of my natural responses. The thawing–out process was very painful, and I often cried to release my dammed–up emotions. I knew I had to find a purpose for my survival, but I did not realise that it would become clear to me only through a crisis which would occur many years later, on the other side of the world.

One day the Matron came into my room and said, 'Betty, I have some news for you, but I want you to keep calm. One of your relatives has survived.'

'It must be a mistake,' I said. 'They are all dead.'

'No, it is not a mistake. It is your husband, he is here.'

I screamed that she was a liar. It could not be. I was told he had died.

'No, Betty, it is true, because he is already here, waiting outside.'

I kept screaming that she was lying. I did not want to see this man. Why wouldn't she leave me alone? Even here, I thought, they will not let me die in peace.

'All right, but I will send him in and you can see for yourself.'

I said, 'I don't want to see anyone,' and buried my head under the blanket.

A voice said, 'Betty, please look up. It's me, really. I have also survived.'

Slowly, carefully, I lifted my head from under the blanket and began to laugh, hysterically.

There was Herman, very skinny, with cropped hair and a puffy face, because he was suffering from starvation oedema.

Matron brought me a sedative and, after a little while, Herman sat beside me and we held hands. We talked about the day of his arrest, two years earlier.

But what had happened to Herman during those two years?

I will let him tell you his own story of survival.

HERMAN'S STORY

CHAPTER EIGHT

AGAINST ALL THE ODDS, I SURVIVED

This is a true account of how, by last-minute reprieves, my own desperate efforts and strokes of great good fortune, against all the odds, I survived. This is a story of war, murder and the abuse of human rights, but also of love, heroism and faith.

I was born in Amsterdam on the 27th of November, 1919, and my brother Sam was born two years later. Ours was a good, middle-class family, and we lived a comfortable life, although we were by no means rich.

Herman and Sam, aged five and four.

Herman's mother, Angelina, with Herman and Sam. Angelina died in Auschwitz in September of 1943.

After graduating from high school I enrolled in night school to study English, French and German. I was also interested in athletics and took my sports training very seriously. Like my father, who was an excellent musician, I played the piano and accordion.

In September 1938, at the age of 19, I was drafted for compulsory military service, and had no trouble being accepted for officer training into the Royal Dutch Air Force. This was no hardship, as all

Herman's grandfather, Hyman Lissing.

Herman's family at the seaside, 1924. From left to right: Angelina (Herman's mother), Jacobus (Herman's uncle), Myer (Herman's father), Sophia (Herman's grandmother) with friends of the family. The children next to Myer are Herman, cousin Max and brother Sam. Jacobus Lissing died in Auschwitz in 1943, Sophia, aged 73, was killed in Auschwitz in early 1944.

Herman in 1939, while in the Royal Dutch Air Force.

of us young men treated our training as a great, exciting game. It was only a year later, when Germany invaded Poland in September 1939, that our attitude changed, because it seemed we might become involved in a war, but it was not until all reserve personnel were mobilised and all leave cancelled that we began to take our training seriously.

Early in 1940 my unit was transferred to the city of Rotterdam. Before long a club for servicemen was established, which soon became a popular meeting place for the young people of Rotterdam. The girls, especially, enjoyed becoming acquainted with soldiers, sailors and airmen. One day a piano arrived and soon I was playing all the latest hits.

Until that fateful day, the 10th of May, 1940, I had a life free of worries. Even to this day I consider my first twenty years to have been good years.

It was 4 a.m., 10th May, 1940. We were asleep in our quarters, in a school converted into army barracks when a continuous drone of planes overhead woke us. I said, 'The Allies are late tonight on their way to Germany.' But then we heard explosions and saw searchlights. It took a few seconds for us to realise that we were being attacked from the air.

The order came for us to dress, and we marched to our headquarters at the Gordelroad, where we heard that the airfield at Waalhaven had been bombed and our combat planes that were stationed there destroyed. Without planes, our division was now attached to the elite corps of the Royal Marines, who had been fighting German paratroopers since early morning. I was put in charge of a section stationed at the Gordelroad, with instructions to watch over and hold the open field adjoining our barracks.

It was now about 8 a.m. German troops were being parachuted on to all open fields and Stuka dive-bombers were attacking Rotterdam with incendiary bombs.

A 500lb bomb hit the roof of the building in which we were stationed, but although it penetrated the top floor, it failed to explode.

Herman's family on a beach outing.

The last picture taken of Herman's family. Herman and I are on the right. Sam with Sophia on left. Little Sophia, daughter of Jacobus, died in Sobibor concentration camp, aged three. Elja, son of Jacobus, was killed in Sobibor too, aged five.

I looked at the large hole in the ceiling, where the menacing bomb was clearly visible. I could hardly believe my luck.

Meanwhile snipers had installed themselves on rooftops and strategic points all over town, and it was our job to apprehend them. We arrested scores of them. Most were Dutch traitors and German civilians who had come to Holland under the pretence of fleeing the Nazis.

It was difficult to find out what was happening in the rest of the country. We knew that gliders and aeroplanes were landing on the speedway to The Hague, and that the country was under water because so many of the dykes had been destroyed in the bombings.

The Marines were engaged in hand–to–hand combat and managed to hold the vital Maasbridge against overwhelming odds, but there was no single front; fighting was going on everywhere in and around the city. By the third day most of our anti–aircraft guns had been silenced. With the airfield in German hands there was no air defence left. Hundreds of Stukas were dropping their bombs everywhere. For the first time in nearly a century, the peaceful population of the Netherlands had to face the agony and destruction of total war.

Fires raged everywhere and for many days, but so many water mains had been damaged that there was no water to put out flames.

The Dutch government had no choice but to surrender to the Nazis. This vicious rape of my beloved Holland by a foreign army was more than I could bear. I cried as I surrendered my weapons. Along with my comrades I was taken prisoner, and crammed into the confined space of a church. From our 'prison' we could see the columns of tanks and armoured personnel carriers which, even after two days and nights, showed no sign of ending.

The German high command was hoping that the Dutch population would recognise their common Aryan heritage, and join them. If there had been even the remotest chance of that happening, the bombardment of Rotterdam and the invasion of our beloved country soon put an end to that. After the German army had passed through on its way to Belgium, (which was already occupied) and France, we were ordered to return to our old barracks, where we would be under house arrest.

A few days later, a vacancy occurred for a courier to carry messages between the various prisons. I volunteered, and was given an old Harley Davidson motorcycle. I knew it was only a matter of time before I would have the opportunity to hightail it out of Rotterdam and rejoin my family in Amsterdam.

And so it came to pass, with papers proving that I was a courier, I managed to talk my way through roadblocks, and was soon riding through the familiar streets of Amsterdam. In all the confusion, I was never missed.

I left the Harley in front of our local police station and considered myself honourably discharged. The Germans did not want to tie up valuable manpower, food or transport keeping war prisoners in

Herman, in uniform, playing the piano at the Air Force base.

Holland, so all Dutch servicemen had been released by the Germans.

When the war was over, and I was again called up for duty, my papers were in order.

Before the war I had been a member of the Amsterdam Athletic Club, and I was their champion 800 and 1500 metres runner, but now, with the Germans issuing decree after decree limiting Jews' movements and forbidding their contact with Christians, I had to find a Jewish sports club. I went along to the famous Bato Gymnastic club, and became a member.

That is where I first met Betty. She oozed health and vitality, as well as being very popular. To my surprise she accepted my invitation for a date.

You know all about our marriage, the loss of our family and our escape from Holland, so let me go on to the day of my arrest by the SS in Brussels.

Because I worked as a musician at night, and had the added security of a musicians' union pass, I was able to move about Brussels as if I had lived there all my life. I was free during the day, and so started to carry messages for the Belgian resistance.

On the afternoon of the 10th of August 1943, I was walking home, carrying a large fruit pie for our evening meal, when I heard someone calling my name. I looked around and recognised two friends from Amsterdam who had come out of hiding to buy cigarettes. Not knowing where to buy them, they made the mistake of crossing the street to talk to me.

They did not know that they had been followed by a car carrying Gestapo agents looking for escaping Jews. They stopped beside us, their pistols drawn. The fact that I ran, and they had to chase me through several streets before they caught me, did not help my situation. We were all taken to Gestapo headquarters. That evening, after hours of interrogation and beatings, I was taken to the notorious Gestapo prison on Avenue Louise, where I was separated from my friends because, according to my papers, I was a Belgian Christian, whom the Nazis suspected of being a spy and a member of the Resistance.

I was interrogated and beaten again, as they felt sure that I knew where other spies were hiding, before I was thrown back into my cell, bleeding, with blackened eyes and longing for Betty, who was always composed and a tower of strength. I thought of all the people who had risked their lives to help us, and all the agonies we had already endured to escape. I cried myself to sleep.

When I woke next morning I noticed a message had been scratched onto the concrete wall with a nail. It read: 'To all who dwell here, COURAGE. We will be victorious'.

I found a piece of glass and scratched on the wall, 'Herman Lissing has been here,' using my own name for the first time since leaving Amsterdam. (Visiting Brussels after the war, I went to that prison, to see my old cell. The messages were still on the wall.)

I was taken into a large room where three SS officers interrogated me. When I refused to answer their questions, one said, 'We are wasting time. He does not want to talk. Shoot him.'

I started to talk, but I did not tell them what they wanted to hear. I told them the truth, that I was a Jew from Amsterdam who was trying to escape to England.

'It makes no difference, the death sentence still stands.'

'Why waste a bullet, there is a transport with Jews leaving tomorrow, let him be on it. In Auschwitz he will die anyway.'

This remark gave me the first indication of where I was going and what could happen to me. However, I must have been one of the very few Jews whose life has been saved by being Jewish.

I was taken to Malines transit camp where, together with 1200 others, I was to stay for the next six weeks, waiting transport to Auschwitz. I received mail and a food parcel from Betty, so I knew she was in contact with Jo Panke.

SS soldiers were stationed inside and outside the camp,and all the prisoners were locked in their quarters before nightfall. During the day prisoners were allowed to go outside into a large courtyard, but always under heavy guard.

Food was bad, but not limited in any way and, apart from domestic chores, no work was expected from the prisoners. It did cross our minds that if conditions were like this in German camps, we, the young people, would be able to survive.

Suddenly, on the 19th of September 1943, without any prior warning we were ordered to line up in the courtyard. Under heavy guard we were marched to a waiting train of cattle wagons, and handed over to a company of SS officers and soldiers. They used their rifle butts and batons to push us into the cattle trucks and we were locked in. Without food or water we started the death ride to Auschwitz.

Women, children, babies, old people—all were packed together in complete darkness, with no room to sit, lie down or even stand comfortably, for three, sometimes four or more days.

The fanaticism of the SS can be measured by the fact that even German troops on their way to the front sometimes had to wait for days before transport was available. But the transports taking Jews, Gypsies, clergy and opponents of the Nazi regime to the death camps were always ready. Our extermination had priority over winning the war.

There is nothing that I can think of that degenerates people faster than to deny them toilet facilities, water and food, and lock them in a dark and confined space. If I thought our transport was inhumane, however, I would soon learn that it was only the first in a long series of horrendous experiences.

There had been nothing in my life – me, the ex Air Force officer, champion athlete, healthy, modern twentieth–century man – to prepare me for the absolute misery, the senseless cruelty that I would have to endure for the next twenty months.

People often use the expression 'hell on earth', perhaps without really understanding the full meaning of what they are saying. I, for one, can talk about hell on earth with authority, because I have been there. I also know that there are no words in any vocabulary to describe the utter agony and despair inflicted upon their victims by the German Nazis.

Stumbling out of the cattle truck, I was prodded with a rifle butt towards a group of men in white coats sitting behind long tables. Each of us had to file past that table and from there on to the waiting trucks. A few young men were told to step aside and form another line.

About a hundred of us were marched, under heavy guard, towards a row of barracks in the distance. On our way we were passed by trucks carrying the rest of our transport, and we watched them turn towards the buildings with smoking chimneys.

Being chosen to work, I found out, was not a guarantee of being spared from the gas chamber. Selection for death could come at any moment. I soon learned that nobody cared whether we lived or died. The struggle to stay alive on one scoop of watery soup made from potato peels, and a piece of mouldy bread, was so constant and so intense, that compassion for other prisoners was practically impossible.

Our 'work' consisted of breaking large stones with sledge-hammers, behind the barracks.

After roll call, we had to witness the hanging of two 'saboteurs', who had stolen some food from the garbage tip behind the kitchen. Hangings from this 'crime' took place almost every day.

Apart from the ever present hunger, we also had to cope with vermin. Every variety of bug and lice bit into our starved flesh. Nobody could escape. In the few hours of free time we were granted, it was sometimes possible to shower and try to keep clean. Without washing regularly, the vermin on our bodies increased. When a person stopped washing himself, he was on the verge of becoming a *Musselman* – a walking skeleton, doomed to die.

Behind the washroom was a market where prisoners gathered to exchange and barter their meagre goods. Food was the magic word. Men would argue for hours about the value of a piece of bread, or a cigarette or a piece of cloth which could be used as a sock. Everything had a use. Even an old newspaper could be used as an undergarment around the chest, to keep the icy cold wind a little bit at bay.

Because I could speak German and French, I learned that the smaller camps had no gas chambers, or selections. Of course there was still hard labour, but the chance of survival was better than in a destruction camp, a camp such as Auschwitz.

One day after returning to my barracks after work and roll call, I was ordered to go to the clothing store. There, to my surprise and comfort, I was given a warmer set of clothing. I was then ordered back to the camp square where twenty of us, escorted by four SS guards and two *Kapos* with dogs, were marched out of the camp. We were going to work in a coal mine at Furstengrube.

HERMAN'S STORY

CHAPTER NINE

LABOUR IN THE COAL MINE

The weather was mild, and it was a relief to get away from the continual stench of burning bodies. It took about six hours to reach the camp at Furstengrube. What I noticed immediately was that the prisoners here were more warmly dressed and better fed. There was also a small barrack called the *muzik Stubl* (music hall).

The work in the mine was hard, and we were supervised by the local coal miners. Their treatment of the prisoners was fair, providing we did our work.

One Sunday the *Laager Alteste*, the camp leader (not to be confused with the camp commandant, an SS officer), came up to me and said, 'I have been informed that you are a musician. Can you play the piano accordion?'

'Yes.'

'Good. I have been looking for someone with whom I can play, as I am a professional drummer. I will arrange some concerts for the guards and possibly also for the prisoners.'

And that is what happened, and my daily existence improved to an almost bearable level. I still had to work in the coal mine, but playing in the *muzik Stubl* earned me extra food, which helped me to get stronger.

One day the *Laager Alteste* said to me, 'You don't have to work in the mine any more. From now on you will look after the music room.'

I had now the status of a 'prominent', still a prisoner, but on the same level as a *Kapo*, and this could make the difference between living and dying.

In the music room was a piano accordion, a drum set and various violins and guitars. My responsibilities were to keep the room clean and look after the instruments. The music room was also the temporary home of Tita, the camp commandant's dog, because she had just given birth to a litter of puppies.

I was terrified of the vicious German Shepherd, but fortunately Tita was tied up, and when cleaning the room I made sure to stay out of reach of her and her puppies. She snarled and growled every time I came into the room but, after a while, she became used to me, and gradually accepted me as a friend. I also lost my fear of her, and she allowed me to hold her puppies.

Life in Furstengrube was exactly what it was supposed to be – a work camp for forced labour. But there were no gassings, and we could live without the constant fear that each moment could be our last, unlike in Auschwitz–Birkenau.

I became known as *der Musiker* (musician) and even the soldiers sometimes slipped me extra bread or potatoes. The next six months enabled me to build up some reserves of strength, which I was going to really need.

One day, after I had been in the camp for six months, a truck on the way to Auschwitz with about 40 'selections' broke down not far from Furstengrube. The doomed prisoners were marched into our camp to wait while repairs were carried out. Among them I recognised an old friend from Amsterdam, Salomon van Cleef, a violinist of note.

While the guards were distracted by a noise, I took Sal into my barracks and hid him in my bunk. It was my idea to let him have one comfortable night, as it was bitterly cold outside, but when we went outside the next morning the truck, with the other 'selections' was on its way to Auschwitz. How Sal had been missed during the roll call could only have been due to the free–flowing beer that the guards had consumed the night before.

I knew I was in big trouble. I sent Sal back to my bunk while I stood roll call. When the guards made their usual inspection of the barracks they found Sal, and an inquiry was ordered. Seeing that the situation was hopeless, I confessed that I was responsible for Sal being in the camp, but I had only been trying to save an old friend, who was also a first–class musician, and could be of value to the camp orchestra.

Sal, who had only followed my lead, was allowed to stay in Furstengrube and join the orchestra. I was to be punished and sent back to the coal mine. Only the fact that I was *der Musiker* had saved me from execution.

Punishments were always carried out on Sundays, so as not to interfere with the work load. This was only Tuesday, so I had time to reflect on my fate. Whatever my punishment would be, it would certainly result in physical damage, and not being able to work meant death.

On Sunday the entire camp was assembled to see me punished.

After roll call my number was called, and I knew my time had come. In my agony I had not noticed it was snowing heavily and an icy wind was blowing. My fellow prisoners were cursing me for being the reason they were standing outside in a snowstorm.

As soon as I came forward, I was stripped naked, the camp commandant grinned, and blew a whistle, calling his killer dogs. Within seconds a vicious Doberman had hold of my arm. Two other dogs were slavering on their leads. Once they joined the Doberman, they would soon finish me off. Tita was called out for exercise but she recognised me, and growled at the Doberman, chasing him away. She came back to me and licked my face, as if to say to the other dogs, 'This is my friend, so lay off.'

The Commandant said, 'You are the luckiest b––––– in this camp,' and called off the punishment.

However, I knew that something else was going to happen to me. The SS would not allow me to go unpunished. Their entire system was based upon meting out punishment, so it could instil fear.

A few weeks later, I was told to collect my meagre possessions: one bowl, one piece of soap, one spoon and a vest, given to me by a friend in Auschwitz.

A truck with other 'selections' arrived in the camp. Before I got on board, Sal came up to me and said, 'I am partly to blame. Let me talk to them.'

'No, Sal. You know they will not change their minds.'

As I sat in the truck I tried to come to terms with saying farewell to life.

After about an hour's drive, the truck suddenly stopped. The doors were thrown open and with the usual shouts of *Raus, Raus* (Out, Out), we were lined up beside the truck.

I believed that we had arrived at Auschwitz, but as I looked around I could not see the dominant feature of that camp, the smoking chimneys. Risking a beating, I turned to the *Kapo* guarding us and asked, 'Which camp is this?'

He answered, 'This is Camp Monowitz, the camp for the works at Buna–I.G. Farben Industries.'

As he was concentrating on his task of guarding us, he forgot to hit me for my impertinence in asking a question without first getting his permission.

We were left standing for at least an hour and, although we could not be sure of having escaped the death we thought awaited us, a flicker of hope started to stir inside us. Usually, there were no stopovers on the way to the gas chambers. I could not think of a single reason why we would be treated differently from the many thousands who had preceded us. I only knew that whatever the reason was, it certainly was not compassion. However even a few hours of life were a bonus, and we accepted the delay gratefully.

It was the first day of April 1944, and my second wedding anniversary.

HERMAN'S STORY

CHAPTER TEN

THE BUNA FACTORIES

We had arrived at Buna–Monowitz, the camp supplying labour for the work force of the I.G. Farben Industries. The works were situated within twenty minutes' walk of the camp, and every morning thousands of prisoners would march out of the camp, accompanied by the sounds of the camp's orchestra. Actually, the camp had been purposely built at that particular spot to accommodate the works for the Buna factories. It was also only seven kilometres from Auschwitz, so a constant supply of labour was assured.

After being registered, we were told to report to Block 10. Only then did we realise we had escaped (for the time being at least) the gas chamber. We did not dwell on the questions of why and how, but just accepted gratefully the fact that we were still alive.

The layout of the camp was very similar to Auschwitz, with the notable exception of the lack of crematorium. The conditions at Buna were slightly better than those at Auschwitz, and most prisoners were able to work. We still had to stand in line outside the block in a temperature well below zero. Dressed in rags, we were soon covered with snow.

Buna was a huge complex of factories, all working for the war industry. The camp had been built to supply labour to the factories and that was the reason for our 'miraculous' escape. The day before there had been a 'selection', depleting the ranks and necessitating the recruiting of labour. Not only prisoners worked at Buna, but also hundreds of 'civilian' workers from all the occupied countries, and even English prisoners of war.

At noon a siren sounded for 'lunch'. There were canteens and messrooms for all the civilians and soldiers, but we prisoners had to stay where they were. We did however get a bowl of thin cabbage soup, our daily ration of food when working.

To walk from the camp to the factory was a new experience for us, as we passed civilians and even children, all free and doing what normal people everywhere were doing. When we marched back to the camp after a day's work, however, we were brought right back to the cruel reality of being prisoners with no rights whatsoever, not even to life itself.

As the factories were closed on Sunday, we prisoners stayed in the camp. That did not mean we had a day of rest. We had to unload heavy bags of cement from trucks.

My resistance and general health were deteriorating rapidly, and I suddenly lost all will to go on. I dragged myself to the hospital, where I was allocated a bunk and prepared myself to go with the next selection.

The next morning I was awakened by someone pulling me by the arm.

'There is someone outside who claims he is one of your family.'

I slowly climbed down from my bunk and stumbled outside, where I fell into the arms of my brother Samuel, who had just arrived from another camp and learned that there was a relative of his in the hospital. The sight of Sam suddenly gave me a renewed will to live and I left the hospital immediately.

My brother kept saying, 'You look like a walking skeleton.'

Sam had just arrived from a camp in Holland, where conditions were much better than in the German camps. Being a diamond cutter, he had received special treatment and, together with others from the diamond industry, was employed by the Nazis to cut diamonds. He had been reasonably well-fed and, under the circumstances, looked good.

To be able to see Sam and talk to him regularly gave me renewed hope of staying alive, but one day, when I came back from work, I learned that Sam, along with the other diamond cutters, had been sent to Auschwitz.

I was devastated. I didn't even get a chance to say goodbye.

So I was alone again, working at a clearing site, shovelling stones and dirt. One morning I was told to join another *Kommando*, a group which was working on the construction of a bridge which was to connect two factories.

I had to sit on top of a sort of 'painter's donkey', suspended about eight metres above the ground, and tighten heavy nuts and bolts with a huge spanner.

One morning, while working on the bridge I fell asleep from sheer exhaustion. I slept there on the platform, with everyone looking up to see when I would fall from my high perch. I did not hear the *Meister* (boss) call out to me, until finally he had to send up another worker to wake me.

When I came down, the *Meister* informed me that he had put my number in his book and would report me for committing sabotage. This meant certain death. Sabotage was punished by hanging or by being flogged with a baton, one metre long and two centimetres thick. This punishment was carried out in the 'bunker' – an underground cell, where prisoners were tortured.

Every camp under Nazi control had a punishment bunker.

I knew that 25 strokes with the baton meant a broken spine and smashed kidneys. Surviving the punishment was a useless and painful experience, as the victim generally either died within a few days, or was sent to the gas chamber.

I looked at the *Meister*. I knew the situation was hopeless. I felt violently sick and started to gasp for air. He told me to sit down as I could not work anyway.

At noon the siren sounded for the meal break, as usual.

But this time it did not stop, it just continued. This was unusual. But then we heard the sound of aeroplanes approaching. This was the first time an air raid had taken place over Buna. Bombs began to fall and the SS and civilians took cover. We prisoners had to stay where we were. For about 40 minutes wave after wave of aircraft flew over. They concentrated on the nearly finished factories, which we were connecting with bridges. The air raid destroyed one of the new factories, but did no damage to Buna.

When the 'all clear' sounded, there were only a few casualties, one of whom was the *Meister*. He lay buried beneath a pile of rubble, with my number in his pocket. It was never found, and without minimising my other near misses, I consider this episode as my closest brush with death.

HERMAN'S STORY

CHAPTER ELEVEN

THE LONG ROAD TO FREEDOM

From that day on I was convinced that I would survive the camp, as I could not imagine a closer call.

After the bombardment of Buna and with the Russians getting ever closer, a change seemed to come over the Germans. Some became more talkative and approachable, others even more embittered and sadistic.

One thing was sure, the Germans were facing defeat, and the question which concerned us was whether we would come out alive or dead. There were no illusions as to what the SS intended. They could not afford to leave any evidence of their cruelty and inhumanity.

Less and less work was being done at Buna, and sabotage became more and more common.

On the 17th of January, 1945, we were told at roll call that no work would be done that day, and that inspections would be made in all barracks. Almost at the same time, we could hear artillery fire in the distance. It became clear that the Russians were very close.

There was a certain excitement in the atmosphere, as it was evident that something dramatic would happen. Perhaps even liberation by the Russians.

After being locked in our barracks for 24 hours, we were again ordered out for roll call. We could not believe the sight that met our eyes.

All the civilian kitchen staff, all the musicians, all the SS guards, in short everyone who would normally stay behind in the camp when we went to work, were also lined up.

The SS were heavily armed, with large packs on their backs. At the end of the line were dozens of trucks, carts, a light cannon and even two large Tiger tanks. There were SS men on horseback, and even bicycles, and a column of Wehrmacht infantrymen made up the rear.

Kapos went along the lines of prisoners, handing each of us a full loaf of bread, saying, 'This is the only food you will get for the next three or four days. We don't know when or where we will get the next supply.'

Of course, we now realised the entire camp was being evacuated. To where and to what fate were the questions, not only for us prisoners, but for most of the SS as well.

It was a cold and miserable day, with snow more than half a metre deep, and an icy wind blowing. The SS kept urging us to go faster and faster as we moved out of the camp. Of course, the SS guards were not common soldiers who had been drafted or stationed at the camps by chance. They were volunteers, well aware of what they were doing. They had all been trained in special units and had no desire to fall into enemy hands, especially those the Russians, as there were many Russian prisoners in the German camps, Christians as well as Jews.

This journey was a Death March. The SS shot anyone who could not keep up and the road was strewn with bodies.

Without a moment's rest, we covered 180 kilometres, without food or water. Nobody wanted to be in the last section of the column as those ran the biggest risk of being shot, so there was a constant pushing forward by desperate people. Prisoners would take the clothes and rations of the fallen. It was either that or perish.

All the time an icy wind froze our hands and feet and soon the intense cold started to take its toll of even the strongest. By the hundreds, people just sat down and could not get up again. They either froze to death before the SS could reach them or were shot.

Eventually we neared the road from Auschwitz–Birkenau, and there saw the same thing happening as in Buna–Monowitz. The entire population of Auschwitz was waiting to join our pathetic group and, together with prisoners from other camps, we must have numbered between 60 000 and 80 000 people. We were the last surviving concentration camp inmates in that area.

The struggle for life, and the hunger and agony we endured in the hope of being one day free again, made the death march a calamity. With no let up, we were driven ever faster by the guards, who were by now themselves in a panic.

It was clear from the sounds of the Russian cannonfire that we were only just ahead of them. At last we reached an abandoned camp, Gross Rosen, near the town of Gleiwitch. Because this camp's layout allowed a large number of prisoners to be secured by the least number of guards, we were all driven inside and packed together like sardines.

Prisoners, guards and *Kapos* from various camps were now all thrown together, and there was complete chaos. The *Kapos* had lost their authority and were now treated the same as other prisoners. Some of these *Kapos* had for years been bestial toward their fellow prisoners, so it was no surprise that a few of them had fatal accidents during the night.

The SS did not trust anyone and ruled by terror. Human life was worth absolutely nothing, and people were being shot dead just for tripping over a stone.

In all the turmoil I saw a familiar face. I could not put a name to that face, but its owner also recognised me. We kept staring at each other, and suddenly he said, 'You are Herman Lissing, Betty's husband. Don't you recognise me? I'm Betty's cousin, Sally Wynschenk.'

Now I knew how utterly emaciated we all were. Sally used to be one of the best and fittest boxers in Holland. He had come with a column from Auschwitz and told me the first good news I had for years. He had seen Betty. She had been marched out of Auschwitz with the rest of the inmates of the women's camp.

She must have been within only a few kilometres of us, but it might as well have been a thousand, for all the good it did me.

I had only to look around, and the ray of hope sparked by the news of Betty being alive faded. From what I could see, there was no chance that anyone would survive this hell much longer.

During the afternoon of the following day we were chased out of the barrack, where we had tried to sleep. Huddled together in the yard, Sally and I clung together, scared of losing each other.

Hours later, we had to line up in long rows, packed together like sardines.

As the order came to start moving, I heard my name being whispered. I looked around and could not believe my eyes. There was Sal van Cleef and a whole group of people I knew from Furstengrube walking just behind me. They had taken the same route as us and now had joined the larger columns from Auschwitz-Birkenau and Buna-Monowitz. Ignoring the risk of being punished for breaking rank, they all wanted to talk to me, as they had been sure I would have been gassed within an hour of leaving Furstengrube.

When I told them that we had no food whatsoever, they gave me some bread, which I shared with Sally. The prisoners from Furstengrube had at least been given a little bit more to eat, as the commandant had ordered all the food from the kitchen to be distributed equally. That was the one and only gesture of humanity I encountered in a Nazi all the time I was held in a concentration camp.

As we walked out of the camp, we were ordered to the side of the road and commanded to halt. In the distance, I saw a long row of women prisoners approaching. I thought that by now I was used to anything, but the sight of these women with their shaven heads, sunken chests and stick-like arms and legs, many of them without teeth, was like something out of a horror movie.

We were marched to a railway siding, where we had to board a similar train to the one which had brought me to Auschwitz. Now we began another trek, into Germany on a cattle train to an unknown destination. There were trains pulling out from everywhere, as by now the front was closing in. Everything and everyone the

Wehrmacht had left to fight with was being sent back to Germany for the final stand.

This time, however, the wagons were open and we had no protection from the snow and the ice. We froze. I saw people with their limbs frozen to each other, dying joined together like Siamese twins. I saw people die with foam on their lips, desperate from the effort of trying to break loose from frozen bodies.

After three days, during which the only food we had was morsels thrown into the wagons by passing civilians, we arrived at a large, well–lit camp, into which we marched, now only a pitiful 1500 or so. That was all that was left of the 4000 who had boarded the train.

Camp Dora was different from the other camps. Here the forced labourers and prisoners worked on the V2 rockets.

After standing roll call for hours, we were marched into a large barrack called the *Kino* (cinema). We were all crammed into a totally inadequate space. On the stage we found buckets of water, and a few drums of boiled unpeeled potatoes.

I did not join in the stampede to get to the stage, as I was too weak, and I had Sally to look after. By now he could no longer stand. I had no illusions about what would happen to us. We would be left to die. I started to look around for a way to get out of this hell hole.

Looking out of one of the window slits, I saw a civilian gesturing to me to break the window and climb through.

He spoke French and this was where all those French lessons paid off. He told me to squeeze through the narrow window which, as I only weighed 94 lbs, was not difficult. I called Sal van Cleef, who also managed to squeeze through, but there was no way we could get Sally out. I never saw him again.

We followed the Frenchman to his barrack. He gave us some food and he pointed to some empty bunks, where we laid down and rested.

I could not sleep, my mind full of images of the death march, the agonised suffering experienced by so many thousands, the inhumanity of the Germans. Even now I cannot find adequate words to describe the horror. But there are still moments when I want to scream at the heavens.

There was no proper roll call at the camp, but to remain undiscovered would be impossible, so we stood roll call with our French protector, and Sal and I were marched out of Dora to a small work camp, called Ricklimgen. It was quite different from other camps as it housed mainly *Kapos*, political prisoners and forced labourers.

For the next few weeks we had to lay tracks for a new railway line with no train in sight. The guards kept shouting 'Faster, faster' and one would have thought that only our efforts to lay this line for a non–existent train would save the Fatherland. But that was typical of the Nazi mentality.

One morning we noticed that there were very few guards left in the camp. They lined us up without roll call, which was also unusual, and marched us off. Sal and I looked at each other, hardly daring to hope, as we could hear small arms fire not far off.

Coming to a clearing in the wood, we were ordered to sit down. In the distance, we could see a column of tanks, approaching rapidly. The Germans had very few tanks left, and we were all sure that these belonged to the Americans.

Sal and I, the only two Jewish prisoners, kept very much to ourselves, but we were all very silent, and some of the other prisoners were praying. I looked around, fearing the guards were going to shoot us, but they had all fled.

I found out later that the guards in all the camps had orders not to leave a single prisoner alive, but in our case the rapid advance of the Americans frightened our guards, who ran off leaving their weapons behind.

Suddenly we could see a military column of trucks and tanks across the wheatfields, moving parallel to our position. The white star painted on each vehicle was clearly visible.

We started to shout and wave our arms and before long a truck came towards us across the wheatfield. Three American soldiers jumped out, one of them shouting, 'What are you guys doing here?

You are sitting bang in the middle of the combat zone.'

But as he got closer to us, his face suddenly turned white and he just stared. I approached our liberators and said, in English, 'I have been waiting a long time for you to come. Please help us, we have suffered so much and we are near the end of our endurance.'

One of the men opened his arms and hugged me.

I was liberated.

It was Friday the 13th of April, 1945.

After giving us cigarettes, chocolate and all the rations they had with them, the Americans told us to stay put, and ambulances would come and take us to hospital.

They kept on repeating, 'Jesus, how is this possible? What have they done to these people?'

Heavy fighting surrounded us, and the horizon was aflame as if a huge fire was burning. But about an hour or so later a row of ambulances came across the wheatfield. Without any fuss, the orderlies laid us gently on stretchers and took us to a small church, which had been converted into an emergency hospital.

Being the only one of our group who could speak English gave me a moral lift. I was, of course, near collapse, but somehow I found renewed energy. The Americans were very well-equipped, and before long food was being prepared for us. Pancakes made from milk powder and cans of hash potatoes provided us with the first decent meal we had eaten in years. With my stomach full, and speaking my best English, I walked around like a king.

In a far corner of the church was an old organ, and I suddenly found the strength to start playing. Soon all the Americans were singing away, and it reminded me of how I used to play for my Air Force mates in Holland. Although that was only five years ago, it seemed to have been in another life, so long, long ago.

The next morning we were loaded into trucks, the worst cases travelling in ambulances, and we set off for Hanover, 400 kilometres away.

When we arrived at the hospital, there were no vacant beds, as many wounded German soldiers and civilians had been brought in. Of course there was no room for any concentration camp survivors. An American colonel and his two aides marched into the hospital and demanded to see whoever was in charge. When the superintendent arrived, the colonel drew his pistol and said, 'If an empty ward is not available in ten minutes, I will personally shoot you and your staff.'

The superintendent went on his way and within ten minutes we were bedded down in our own ward.

It took some time, but Sal and I gradually became stronger and we wanted to get back to Holland as soon as possible. We had to wait for transport, however, so while we still slept and ate at the hospital, we were able to move about the town freely. And that was something to savour.

Finally a transport train was due to leave for Holland.

It was explained to us that the journey would not be very comfortable, but we would be provided with food and drink, we would not be cramped, and there would be frequent stops. Compared to our other train journeys, it would be luxurious. We left the next day for Holland and, seeing the destruction and havoc that the war had caused, I began to realise that I was not the only one to suffer.

We arrived at the Dutch border late in the afternoon. We were the first prisoners and forced labourers to return to Holland. As soon as we reached the border, long rows of people waving the Dutch flag and singing the national anthem gave us an unforgettable welcome. In the centre of the city of Eindhoven, a hall had been converted into a reception centre where we had to present our Displaced Person cards, which we had been given before leaving Germany.

Inspections were very thorough, as the authorities were well aware that unwanted persons might try to sneak in under the guise of being prisoners. When the truth about the concentration camps was made known to the Dutch people, they opened their homes and took in anyone who was without shelter. A kindly couple, Mr and Mrs Vroegop, took me into their home and for the first time in two years, I had a really hot bath, and went to bed with clean sheets and a pillow.

Every day I went to the information centre to inquire about my relatives and pored through the list of survivors. One morning a lady from the information centre came to the Vroegops' home to tell me in person that a Betty Lissing, née Wynschenk, had been reported as a survivor, and had entered the country through the reception centre at Enschede. This town was approximately 120 kilometres north of Eindhoven, and at this point in time impossible to reach. There was no transport and three large rivers to cross. I thought that perhaps Betty might go to Amsterdam.

One day, having been told that a truck was going to try to get through to Amsterdam, I said goodbye to the Vroegop family and was on my way.

When we arrived at the railway centre in the city, we were surrounded by hundreds of people all shouting the names of their relatives. As yet they had not heard the terrible truth. Not one of the 30 survivors on the truck had the heart to tell them what had happened to over 100 000 Jews from Amsterdam.

I had an uncle in Amsterdam, who had married a Christian lady. I rang him from the station and heard his very excited voice on the phone. I ran to one of the drivers and begged him to take me to my uncle's home, which was not far from where we were. After the initial emotional greetings, my first question was, 'Have you heard from Betty?'

He had, and she was in a rest home, a converted castle near Ommen. She was very ill, and in no condition to be moved. I decided I would get to Ommen, which was on the other side of the country, even if I had to walk.

A few days later on a borrowed bicycle, I started on my journey. I kept up a steady pace, and by the afternoon I had reached the city of Utrecht. I realised it would take me three or four days to reach my destination, and I was still pretty weak, so I stowed the bicycle in a safe place from where I could later recover it and started to thumb rides. By the next afternoon I had reached the town of Zwolle, which was only about 20 kilometres from Ommen. There was, however, a 100–metre wide, fast–flowing river between me and Betty. I tried to find a way across, but without success.

It was all very frustrating. I had survived the hell of Auschwitz, yet a single river prevented me from seeing my beloved wife again. Just as I was beginning to contemplate the possibility of swimming across, I saw a police launch berthing a little way upstream from me. I yelled at the policeman behind the wheel to listen to me. When I explained my mission, and where I had come from, he took me on board and made an extra crossing, a kindness for which I will be forever grateful.

HERMAN'S STORY

CHAPTER TWELVE

AGAINST ALL ODDS

REUNION

The rest of my journey was easy. I finished my trip by riding on top of a milk wagon, pulled by an old horse.

Just outside of Ommen I saw a sign, 'Road to Castle Eerde'. That was where Betty was being nursed. I walked through the big gates, up a long drive, and came to a lawn, where people were resting on beds and stretchers.

I walked up the steps, and as I entered the hall a woman approached me. I told her my name and that I had been told my wife was here. She became very agitated and said, 'Oh my God, this is a miracle. Your wife is here, and she is very ill, she has no will to live. She does not eat and will not speak to anyone. Now with you here, it is possible that this will change. You cannot go in and catch her unprepared, as the shock might be too much for her.'

She took me by the hand and led me to an adjoining building, where she left me in the hall and told me to wait until she came to get me.

That is how Betty and I were reunited. We had survived the brutality, the gas chambers, the starvation and thirst, the snow and ice. Not even the murderous intent which was the evil platform of the Nazi regime could prevent us from fulfilling our destinies.

Having found each other, we had a reason for living. I was taken in to Castle Eerde as a patient, so I could be near Betty and look after her, and in return I did odd jobs around the place. Time passed

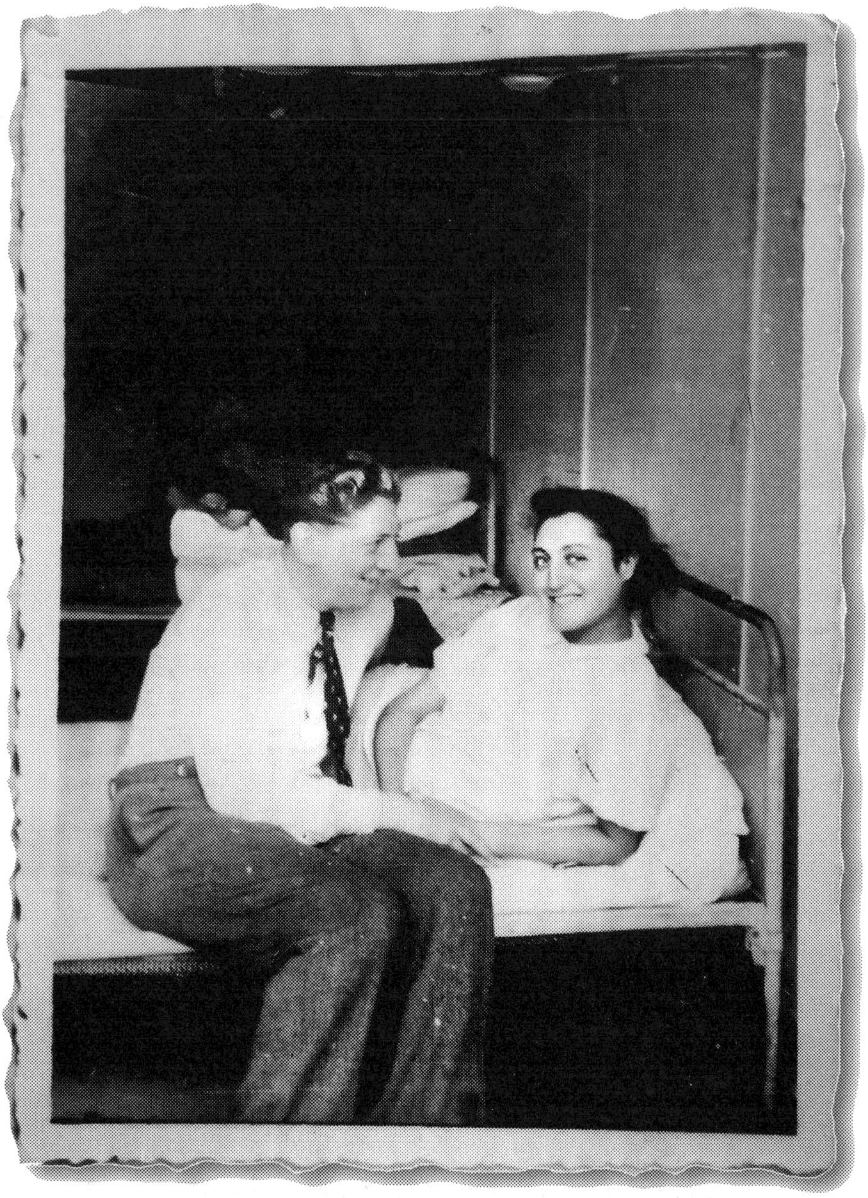

Our reunion at Castle Eerde, 1945, after liberation.

quickly and the good care and tranquil surroundings greatly assisted in Betty's recovery. About four weeks after my arrival, we had another wonderful surprise.

Without any warning, my brother Samuel arrived at Castle Eerde.

He had arrived in Holland via Brussels, which was why his name was not any of the survivors' lists. When he got to Amsterdam he went immediately to see our uncle, found out where we were and came to join us. We began to feel like a family again.

Although we all thoroughly enjoyed the loving care bestowed on us by the matron and the staff at Castle Eerde, we wanted to get back to a normal routine.

I had started to travel to and from Amsterdam regularly, as transport was slowly getting back to normal, so when I was offered a pianist's job in a well-known club/bar in the centre of Amsterdam, I accepted so that I could start to build a new future for us.

Meanwhile, Betty had improved enough to be moved to a regular hospital in Leiden, where she would receive expert treatment for her tuberculosis. It would be another three months before she could come home, during which time she had a miraculous recovery from tuberculosis.

I started to look for a place to live, so that I could receive Betty in style when she came out of hospital. After weeks of looking I was lucky enough to find an apartment in the southern part of Amsterdam.

Our money had lost its value and would soon be replaced by a completely new currency. Cigarettes were the single most important trading commodity, and many Americans who came to the club would tip me in cartons of cigarettes. Being a non-smoker, I was able to exchange them for goods, and that's how I furnished our apartment.

In January 1946, Betty came home, and I was such a proud husband – for the first time since our marriage in April 1942 I could give my wife a home to live in.

But now, to continue our story, here is Betty again.

I was privileged to carry the Bato Club flag at a memorial service held in 1947 for all the members of the Club who did not survive the war.

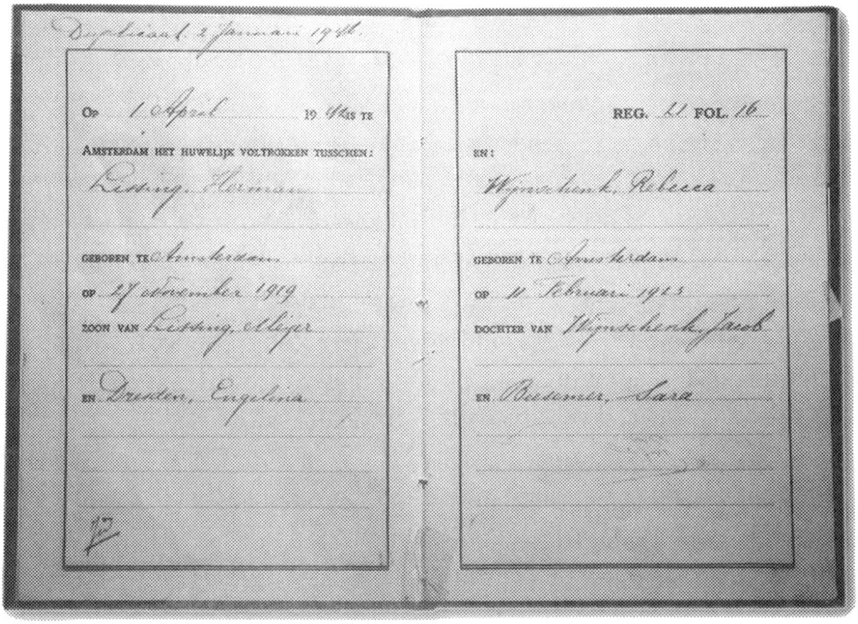

Op 1 April 19   is te
Amsterdam het huwelijk voltrokken tusschen:
Lissing, Herman
geboren te Amsterdam
op 27 November 1919
zoon van Lissing, Meijer
en Drenten, Engelina

Reg.   Fol. 16
en:
Wijnschenk, Rebecca
geboren te Amsterdam
op 11 Februari 1923
dochter van Wijnschenk, Jacob
en Boesman, Sara

A duplicate of Herman and Betty's Marriage Certificate, issued in 1947 after the original had been lost.

CHAPTER THIRTEEN

HOME TO AMSTERDAM

Because Herman's work kept him out at night, I was very much alone, still weak and still under medical supervision.

I began to have terrible nightmares, in which the horrors I had lived through returned to haunt me. While I was asleep, I had no control over my traumas. I could not suppress the horrors of the past years. Time and again, I found myself back in Auschwitz, always in front of the crematorium, waiting to enter. I would wake, paralysed by fear.

What I found most difficult to cope with, was the knowledge that the people I loved so much had been killed. I knew all the details of their deaths, which were pictures that could not be erased from my mind. I had to learn to live with them, and this is something every survivor has to do.

My family doctor, who had looked after me since I was a little girl, made regular visits to monitor my condition, but there was little he could do to ease the grieving process. When my physical condition had sufficiently improved, he suggested that, even at a high risk, I should have a baby. And so I became pregnant, knowing full well the risk I was taking.

When I was three months' pregnant, my doctor gave me permission to visit my cousin, Rebecca, in Brussels. Her husband Jo, her brother Leo, and her father, Joe, had escaped to Spain. From there Jo and Leo had made it to England and joined the Free Dutch Army, which helped to liberate the western European countries. Rebecca had to give her menfolk the terrible news that her mother had been gassed at Auschwitz. Although overjoyed at her survival, like me she was very ill with tuberculosis. She also needed bed rest and good

Herman in his Air Force uniform. He was called up again in 1946 to help with a recruiting drive.

food in order to heal.

When I arrived at her home, I found her in bed.

I said, 'I have a surprise for you. I am three months' pregnant.'

Rebecca answered, 'Wonderful! Now I have a surprise for you, too. I am also three months' pregnant.'

We looked at each other and shared our joy. Our babies were due on the same day. Rebecca later found out that she was expecting twins. Her babies were born five weeks prematurely—a boy and a girl—but unfortunately the boy died after just three weeks. In those days, facilities for premature babies were not good. Thankfully, her daughter lived and now has a family of her own.

Rebecca and I have kept in close touch all these years. We talk about family matters, but never of the past. Rebecca has found it difficult to review her Auschwitz ordeals and prefers to let go by wiping them out of her consciousness.

I can understand that. We each have to deal with our survival in our own way.

With my strong maternal instinct, I had a relatively trouble-free pregnancy. On the first day of November in 1946, I gave birth to a healthy, 4-kilogram baby boy, Martin Louis. Both Herman and I were overjoyed. Our lost families were represented in this precious new life, which helped us immensely.

Becoming a mother gave me the will to live but my nightmares continued. I wept constantly for my family, especially for my mother.

In the meantime, the American soldiers were slowly being transferred to Germany, and the Netherlands Army again took over the command of the country. Many of the clubs opened up for the entertainment of the occupying forces closed down, and there was less work for entertainers and musicians.

When Martin was one year old, Herman was called up again by the Royal Dutch Air Force, because Holland was involved in a conflict in the Dutch East Indies. Herman's job was to help recruit new personnel. He spent a year at the flying base at Ypenburg before he was then relieved of active duty because of his war captivity, but he would remain on the Air Force Reserve List until 1959.

It was very difficult for Herman to readjust to civilian life. We still felt very unsettled, especially with our haunting memories. Although we had a comfortable home, an adorable son and the inexpressible comfort of our joint survival, we could not find peace. We would walk the streets, and look at the houses where our families had lived.

All survivors of the Holocaust in the Netherlands were still in a state of shock. We had to pick up our lives again but, in most cases, there was no-one left to share them with. Other people were not interested in listening to our gruesome stories. They themselves had suffered grievous losses and deprivation at the hands of the Nazis who occupied their country.

In addition, life in Amsterdam was not easy. The city had been completely looted and was devoid of even the most basic necessities.

The first picture of the proud new Lissing family, January 1947. Martin is only three months old.

The Netherlands was still reeling from the effect of the war years, and the process of picking up the threads of post–war life was very slow and painful.

It became obvious to us that we could not rid ourselves of the painful remembrances of our once happy family circle. I remember walking the streets of Amsterdam, always expecting to bump into someone I had known before the war. But so few of them had returned.

It was all more than we could bear, so we began to think of leaving Europe behind us to start a new life. Herman started to make enquiries, first at the American Consulate. As an ex–serviceman he would have no trouble being accepted as an immigrant. However, stateless refugees had first priority and it would take years before we became eligible. After all, we had a good homeland and lived in a democracy.

My first seaside holiday after the war, in 1947. Martin is only seven months old, but already up on his feet. We were on holiday with my girlfriend, Edith.

Martin, aged nine months.

One day we met a friend who had been a sea captain during the war. He had been stationed in Sydney and was full of praise for Australia. In fact, he had plans to settle in Australia permanently, and he convinced us that this was the place for us too. It was a land that needed young people like us, and would welcome us with open arms.

We discussed the possibilities, and Herman sought an appointment with the Australian Embassy in The Hague, where he was told we could get a permit to go if we could pay our own fares. Because he was an ex-serviceman, we would have priority.

Before we left Holland, however, we received the official death notices of the murdered members of our families. These notices stated the exact particulars of the place and date of each death. This information was gathered by the Dutch War Office, and is recorded in the archives of the Dutch Remembrance Committee.

I was particularly broken–hearted when I found that Maurits, my brother, had died on the 20th of March, 1945, just a few weeks before the war's end.

During these post–war years in Holland, I had again joined my old gymnastic club, Bato. It took a very long time for me to get back to my old form, but in 1948 I again took part in competitions in Amsterdam, and won second prize in the national championships.

The club decided to hold a memorial service for all our lost members, at which I was privileged to carry the flag.

A few weeks after our application, we received confirmation of our acceptance as Australian migrants. We would be able to start a new life in a new land.

This is the ship I arrived on, the Volendam, at the Port of Melbourne on Australia Day, 1950.

PART TWO

CHAPTER FOURTEEN

AUSTRALIA

The decision to leave our homeland was made, so that we could begin a new life with Martin, our–three–year–old son.

At that time there was no official government policy assisting immigrants to come to Australia, so when we applied at the Australian Embassy in the Hague, we were told that Herman would have to go to Australia first, so that he could produce a certificate of accommodation for Martin and me.

In September of 1949, having paid our fares, Herman left on the long sea voyage to Sydney. His first priority was to find suitable accommodation, so that he could produce the necessary certificate.

On the 16th of December in the same year, Martin and I left Holland on the SS *Volendam*, bound for Sydney. On the 26th of January, Australia Day, we berthed in Melbourne.

Herman was waiting for us at Port Phillip Bay, where we disembarked. The next day we made the long train journey to Sydney. Herman had found a room with a kitchen in the suburb of Rushcutters Bay. After only six weeks we found a small apartment in the same neighbourhood, and settled down to our new life.

Herman found a job in a big city store, and often had extra work as an interpreter, because of his knowledge of languages. He also played the piano at night to supplement our income, as most of it went on the very high rent.

I enrolled Martin in kindergarten, and he was soon chattering away in English. I also found English easy to learn, and in a very short time was able to do the shopping by myself.

We suppressed our memories as much as possible, and found the relaxed Australian way of life helped us regain some distance from our traumas. The nightmares did not stop, but we carried on if nothing was wrong, as we wanted to provide a balanced and peaceful life for our son.

At the end of our first year in Sydney, a friend who worked for the Department of Immigration asked us if we would like to be interviewed on ABC radio as new Australians, celebrating their first Christmas in Australia. The interview would be used in the King's Christmas message, broadcast by the BBC in London.

Our interview here in Sydney with Keith Smith was duly taped and sent to London.

On Christmas Day, the worldwide broadcast of the message of the King, and of ourselves, was introduced by the actor Robert Donat. On Boxing Day, Herman, Martin and myself appeared on the front pages of most newspapers as the 'The Ideal Migrant Family'.

Our small flat was close to a park and the beach, and I found it relaxing to sit by the water and watch Martin playing. It was a relief to find myself in new surroundings, so that I did not have to deal with the haunting memories of places where I had spent my childhood with family and friends. Had I stayed in Amsterdam, I would have been unable to let go of my happy and carefree pre-war life, and would have found it impossible to start anew.

One morning, I decided to take Martin to nearby Redleaf Pool, to teach him how to swim. As he was playing in the water, he was joined by a little girl about the same age. Her name was Mia.

When it was time for the little girl to go home, her mother came over to fetch her. She looked at me, then came closer. When she saw the number on my arm, she became very excited.

'You were in the Union Munitions Factory at Auschwitz,' she said, 'So was I. My name is Esther Fiszman, and I'm the girl that had her appendix removed in an operation. How did I survive such an experience in that place! I remember seeing you at the factory.'

I did remember this event, and now here we were, both survivors and both mothers, meeting on the other side of the world from the camps.

To this day we keep in touch.

Our first official outing in Australia, to the wedding of a friend's daughter. I made my dress myself, on the sewing machine I had brought with me from Holland and which is still in Martin's possession.

CHAPTER FIFTEEN

NEW FRIENDS AND OLD FRIENDS

We made new friends and became part of a group of former Dutch nationals who held a dance every Sunday night at a restaurant called the 'Black Tulip', where Herman played the piano.

One Sunday night, while I was seated at a table with some friends, the door opened and in walked a middle-aged couple. I looked at the man, and felt I knew him, but I could not place him. He looked at me, and his mouth started to tremble. He stretched out his arms and ran towards me.

'Betty,' he called out, 'My God, you made it.'

Bram Cohen had worked a big press machine in the Union Munitions Factory at Auschwitz. Men and women were not allowed to talk to each other, but as soon as Bram found out that I came from Holland, he often put an extra dish of soup under my machine to supplement my meagre rations. Bram's wife and four children were killed as soon as they arrived in Auschwitz. He knew that if ever he survived the ordeal he would be left alone.

The last time I had seen Bram was at the side of a snow-covered road, when we had been evacuated from Auschwitz on the 18th of January, 1945. When the columns of male prisoners passed us, we had to retreat to the side of the road to allow the men to pass. I crouched, covered by the deep snow, but as usual I called out, 'Are there any Dutchmen?'

'Yes,' said Bram and Sam Lissing, my brother-in-law.

Bram was totally overcome when, in 1951, he saw me sitting at my table in the 'Black Tulip'. He kept saying to me, 'I never thought

I would ever see you again.' Bram had remarried after the war, a war widow, and his new wife was surprised to see her husband become so emotional. She told me later that she thought he had discovered a lost daughter.

Bram died recently, at the age of 94 and at his funeral service, the minister related this incident. He said that of the countless thousands of people on that death march, Bram and myself were destined to survive and meet again in freedom and peace.

The next few years passed peacefully and, to a certain extent, we started to recover. Martin continually asked us why he did not have a brother, so when he was six years old, in 1953, our second son, Jerry, was born. (His given name is actually Jack Monty, Jack after my father and Monty for General Montgomery whom we greatly admired.) We were very content. We felt that the children

Our second son, Jerry, in 1953, when he was six months old.

represented a close link with our lost families. Our sons gave us the strength to carry on.

From a very early age, the boys both had a natural aptitude for sport, which of course we encouraged. We always accompanied them to their sporting fixtures, and the relaxed Australian way of life – picnics, barbeques, cricket, soccer and tennis – was just what we needed in our healing process. I am sure that we were led to Australia for just this reason.

But in 1955 I had a relapse. It was as if the floodgates opened and all the past memories came pouring back, and I had to face again the enormous loss I had suffered through the slaughter of my beloved parents, brothers and close friends. All the pain and turmoil of the war years, that I had tried so hard to repress, could no longer remain hidden, and I found it difficult to function normally.

I battled within myself to find some balance in my life and the reason why I had survived the death camps. A dear Dutch friend, who had just returned from a visit to Holland, gave me *The Diary of Anne Frank* to read. It had just been published in the Netherlands, under the title of *The Attic*.

As I read the book, Anne's description of the events that took place in the hiding place, and her need to express her feelings about her ordeal, inspired me. The courage and faith that developed within her gave me the strength to carry on. Reading about her desire to live on after the war, to tell people about why and how she was forced to hide and live under these circumstances,

Anne Frank

prompted me to relate her story in a series of lectures to high-school students.

Anne has become the symbol of the one and half million children who perished during the Holocaust. Despite the horror of what was happening around and to her, and in the full knowledge of what her fate would be if she was caught by the Nazis, Anne still felt that in his innermost being, Man is essentially good.

I have heard people say, 'Well, Anne made this statement before she experienced the camps, but she would not say this now, if she had survived.'

I feel, within myself, that Anne spoke from an awareness of a deeper dimension, where she knew that people were untouched by conventional ideas of 'good' and 'evil'. This is the reality of mankind's existence on Earth, and Anne's awareness is the secret of her diary's immense impact on humanity. She dreamed of the Brotherhood of Man and knew that one day it would be experienced on earth.

Her indomitable spirit still teaches people to be tolerant and to become aware of the innate good that is within a person's being when he is in tune with his life force. The inspiration I derived from Anne's diary soothed my bruised soul and gave me the courage to proceed with my life.

However the next few years were difficult ones. The nightmares did not cease, and I found myself dreaming of the horrendous experiences I had gone through. During my waking hours I could control my emotions, but as soon as I was asleep they seemed to take over.

I was determined to overcome this pattern, however, as I held to the idea that I must not allow those monstrous Nazis the power to destroy my life. It was then that I embraced the motto, 'Carry on, regardless.'

To this day, that is what I practise. I know from experience that when I feel as if I have reached the limit of my endurance, I can reach into the depths of my consciousness, and from this wellspring I draw an infinite flow of strength. This enables me to continue to face my sometimes insurmountable problems.

In absolute silence the problems often dissolve.

When the play, 'The Diary of Anne Frank', opened in Sydney, I was invited to present the actress who portrayed Anne with flowers in commemoration of the victims of the Holocaust. I was also interviewed on radio and for newspaper articles.

I understood so well the period of Anne's inner growth, which had been accelerated through her forced exile and confinement in a small room. It seems that such conditions often bring forth our truest and deepest feelings.

When I came home after the play I sat down and felt her very near to me. I could do nothing else but put down on paper what I was feeling, which I am sure the reader will understand after reading the following:

> I have just come back from seeing the stage play of 'The Diary of Anne Frank'. I am amazed at how well I know Anne. I can almost feel her spirit and I feel sure that Anne is helping me.
>
> Her diary has given me a different outlook on life, and has also helped me in the struggle to accept life and its complications. Whatever happened in Anne's diary had a unique meaning. And her life and death had a very special purpose to fulfil.
>
> Her father, Otto Frank who was the oldest member of their family, did return from the death camps.
>
> I feel it was meant to be this way. He was the one who had to spread her message amongst people, so that her spirit could go on living and inspire other people. It was her father who could carry out this work for her, because he understood Anne so well. It was also Otto Frank, who was spiritually strong enough to go through the agony of having lost his family and still go on living.
>
> I feel Anne is guiding her father and giving him the strength to bear all the suffering and at the same time educate people to have tolerance for each other.

I really believe that all this was meant to be.

I strongly feel that pain becomes bearable after you realise there is a purpose for suffering.

And I know what pain is. I don't mean the pain when you hurt yourself, but the pain of losing your loved ones.

This is a different sort of pain altogether.

It is then that the soul is hurt, and this hurt never vanishes, but stays with you for the rest of your life. Then you have to learn to live with this hurt and this is not easy.

It is at this time that you need support from God very badly, because if alone, you lose yourself, and start to pity yourself, as I used to do, until I found that I stood not alone.

Then slowly this sort of pain becomes bearable, and you realise there is still beauty left in life.

So you pick up the shattered remains, and begin again with hope in your heart for your children and their children.

You feel that all is not lost and that as long as you live, all your dear ones will live with you. As you grow inwardly, you begin to realise that in death it is only the body that dies. The spirit of the person remains with you. The people you were close to before death took them will remain with you and guide you in all important matters.

I decided to write to Anne's father, to tell him how her diary had helped me and how close I felt to her inspirational story. What Anne brought out in her diary was that, in spite of all the hate and destruction she had experienced, she could still feel the reality of good in people. We can so often learn from the very young.

Otto Frank was very moved to hear how much Anne's diary meant to me, and how much it had helped me in the mastering of my own life. He was very touched that after the sufferings of the war years, I had been faced with the added blow of my little girl being born with Down's Syndrome.

He said that what appeared to be a tragedy instead had led me to a deeper insight in life, and that part of my letter reminded him of a special prayer that was conducted in the synagogue. It reads as follows:

> Let us think of those whom we loved, those who have been taken from us, and gone to their eternal rest. May everything good that they have done, everything beautiful that they have said, be recognised at its full worth, and may we take it as a guiding principle from which we shape our lives.
>
> For thus the living can honour the dead and remain united with them in spirit.
>
> May those who mourn herein, find comfort and draw from it the power of faith in a world inspiring omnipotence, and the immortality of Life.

It is obvious to me how much one individual can influence the world in a positive and uplifting way. The impact that Anne's vision of hope and goodwill has had in the world is well-documented.

Education systems around the world use *The Diary of Anne Frank* to teach her view of humanity, even though she was only 15 when she died in Bergen-Belsen, in March of 1945, just one month before liberation. By leaving her diary behind when she was captured by the Gestapo, she left a counter scenario. She might have perished in Bergen-Belsen, but her spirit remains alive to teach and educate people the world over. That is what she had hoped to achieve, so of course, she triumphed.

I feel that Otto Frank was able to cope with his grief at the loss of his beloved family by passing on his child's message of love and peace to humanity.

Fritzi and Otto Frank in Switzerland, 1969

Otto and Fritzi Frank with Betty and Elinda at the Franks' home in Switzerland, 1969.

CHAPTER SIXTEEN

ELINDA

When I was expecting my third child, I was in poor condition, physically and mentally, as I was still trying to get through this period of reliving the ordeal of the war years.

When I was told that the daughter I had so wanted had Down's Syndrome, the shock stunned me. Medical opinion was that the baby was so handicapped that she was not expected to live, and could not be looked after at home.

Up till then, I had always been able to find a way to solve my problems, but this time there seemed to be nothing I could do about the situation. There appeared to be no care available to help me look after the baby at home. I had reached the limit of my endurance, and I felt I could not go on.

My longing for my parents became unbearable. If only I could have felt their arms around me and the reassurance of their loving concern for my grief at this insurmountable problem.

Herman could not face the situation at all, and did not even want me to go and visit Elinda, who was placed in a nursery for infants born with abnormalities. I was told she could not possibly survive as her general condition was critical. I stayed in bed and cried for a week, until one day I decided to get up and take hold of myself. With that first decision a calmness came over me, and I found the strength to carry on.

No–one could stop me from seeing Elinda at the nursery, but I was only able to visit her twice a week – those were the hospital rules. The staff were rather hostile and could not understand why on earth I wanted to preserve a life that seemed so fragile and weak.

Even Herman found it impossible to accept my determination, but to me this child had great significance.

To me, it was as if this little flame of life had emerged from the ashes of Auschwitz, and I had to nurture that flame and keep it burning until I could bring her home. I knew that once I had Elinda with me, love would do more for her than keep her alive, for love is life's great healing agent.

In the meantime, however, I was called to the nursery often, whenever they thought that Elinda was going to die. A number of times I was asked for funeral arrangements, but I refused, for I always felt sure she would live and come home.

What was so inspiring to me was that during this ordeal a whole new dimension gradually opened up to my awareness. I retreated within myself and concentrated on guidance. Where that guidance was supposed to come from, I did not know. There was no help from outside, and no support to lean on, but nevertheless a calm steadiness came over me, and I felt a joy and reassurance that I had never experienced before.

The thought of 'God' did not enter my mind. Such a concept seemed too abstract, too intangible, too vague to hold on to. If there was a God I did not know Him, and I certainly had no conscious wish to know Him. Yet I felt within myself a 'something'. Such an experience cannot be conveyed in words, but when it happens you know beyond any doubt that you are under its protection, a knowledge that brings you strength and a joyful energy that fills your being. You will never feel quite the same again.

I remember thinking, 'How strange, I never knew anything about such an experience,' but it carries you blissfully forth. You have no choice but to go along for the ride, as I always tell those who are seeking an answer to fill the void within themselves.

I had such need of that inner strength because from all sides I was being discouraged from having so much hope, with the exception of Martin and Jerry, bless them. Our two sons were excited at the prospect of bringing the baby home. To them it was natural that she should be with us. They kept asking, 'When is our sister coming to live with us?' They thought she was beautiful. Such is love in action.

Whenever I visited Elinda, the matron seemed to take delight in showing me the worst cases of deformities at the nursery, as if to discourage my efforts. But nothing could deter me from my conviction that Elinda would live and bring a meaningful purpose to my life.

I searched the world for information on any research on retardation and was led to a clinic in Switzerland that offered a treatment that would improve Elinda's condition. The treatment, in the form of injections, was given by my own doctor. This annoyed matron, but that did not worry me. At thirteen months Elinda was unable to sit up. Five weeks after receiving the first treatment she sat up. Five weeks later, she stood up in her cot, and clapped her hands when she saw me.

Matron said, 'It does not mean anything.'

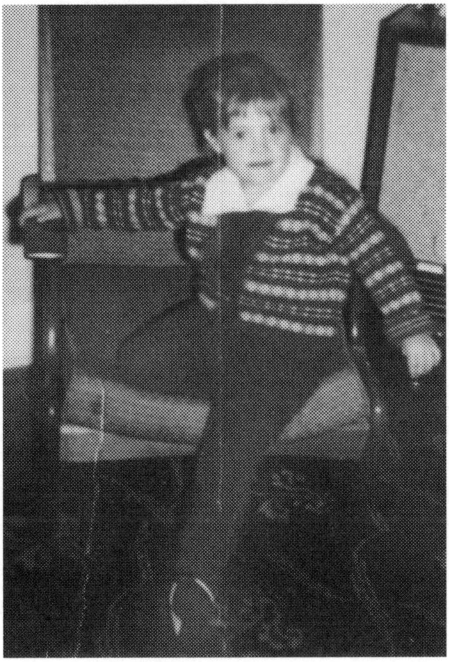

Elinda at age six.

I said nothing but I was ecstatic, because at last Elinda was starting to know me.

Despite the continuing lack of support the 'something' that poured itself through me gave me the courage to carry on. My inner life was revealing itself more and more to me. I became aware of the presence of my beloved family hovering around me. I discovered that they had not really perished but were able to come and comfort me in my time of need. Their bodies had died, not their spirits. I felt I could not speak about this to anyone, however, as it would be too hard to explain in words. Indeed, until it happened to me, I would not have believed anyone telling me of such an experience. So I remained silent, but steadily carried on with my efforts to help my daughter.

When Elinda was 18 months old, Herman and I were allowed to take her out for the day, as by now she had become a bit of a handful for the nursing staff. One evening, when we brought her back to the nursery, we found the matron under the influence of drugs. Out of the blue, Herman decided that we would take the baby home to live with us. To me this was a real miracle, as up to now Herman had thought that having Elinda at home would adversely affect the boys, but taking Elinda home was the first step in uniting us as a whole family.

Herman still found the situation difficult to deal with, as he was also trying to cope with the emotional problems of his war experiences.

It was a lonely journey for me, but one that had to be made. I could only go forward. Old friends dropped away, but I made new friends, who sensed my inner joys and pains, and at the same time I found comfort in their encouragement.

Slowly, Herman let himself become more involved with Elinda. It was wonderful to see the love that she had brought with her take hold in Herman. Over time he became very loving and protective towards her.

One morning he came to me and said, 'I have just written a poem. Do you like it?'

This is what he wrote:

A sun as bright as gold
A sky full of blue and light,
Can feel as chilly cold
And look as dark as night.

For in the human mind
It sometimes may appear,
That all is lost and all's despair
With relief and help nowhere near.
    Yet in the deepest darkness
It is that hope is born,
And understanding and compassion
Bring light that seemed forlorn.
    That like a new born baby
Emerging from its mother's womb,
The sun begins to shine again
And rises from its 'tomb'.

That life again takes meaning
And fears start to disappear,
Skies are becoming blue again
And a feeling of new life is here.

Only then it is said with honesty
That anyone can say,
I really have lived my life in full
Although I have travelled far away.

And now I am contented and happy
Come what may,
For this, dear God, I thank Thee
For this, I humbly pray.

(By Elinda's father)

Professor Paul Niehans, founder of cellular therapy.

In 1969 I took Elinda to a clinic in Switzerland for more treatment. It was not that I was expecting a miracle cure, or that I denied the condition known as Down's Syndrome. What I could not accept was that anything could be termed 'hopeless'.

This was becoming ever clearer to me, as my awareness of an inner-life experience was guiding me, and providing the necessary means to fulfil its plan for me during this earthly journey.

I have learned that we all have a purpose in life. Even the pain we experience in our daily lives, through our unhappiness and failures, can be turned into a positive thing, when we discover that we are not really alone in our struggles. We have inner companions with whom we can connect, and from whom we can receive the guidance we need on how to proceed with our lives.

We often meet the very people we need to help us along, or discover the books that inspire us and help to expand our conscious awareness to a more fulfilling life. One of the joys of life is to meet up with fellow-travellers along the way – people like you and me, who are longing for peace and harmony.

So we made the journey to Switzerland, to give Elinda a better chance of expressing her own purpose in life.

The Swiss treatment consisted of injections of live cells from the organs and tissues of sheep foetuses specially bred for that purpose.

Its pioneer was a very eminent professor, Paul Niehans. He worked on the theory that these cells would activate the under–developed organs of the recipient. His work was based on decades of research in the rejuvenation of organs and tissues.

Many famous people, the whole world over, had received his treatment, which the he claimed helped to delay the adverse consequences of ageing. This same treatment could improve the quality of life for Down's Syndrome children.

Although the Professor was by now in his eighties, he had only just retired from active practice and had trained specialists to continue his work. I was privileged to be invited to the Professor's home in Vevy. He sent his limousine and chauffeur to the Clinic to bring me to his home. We spent a number of hours talking about his research and his struggle to have his treatment recognised by the medical establishment.

It was the most memorable event in Elinda's treatment. He gave me a lot of information about the results of his treatment on Down's Syndrome children. Later, when a book was published about the Professor's life and work, I found there was a chapter on Elinda and me.

When I returned to Sydney, I handed many of the Professor's clinical reports to an eminent endocrinologist in Sydney. When the time came for Elinda to have further treatment this professor volunteered to administer the injections, without charge. What a blessing that I found someone willing to listen and learn from something hitherto untried in medical treatment.

I am forever grateful that Elinda has never been deprived of anything that could help her to further develop.

Before I left Australia with Elinda in 1969, I had told Otto Frank when I would be in Switzerland, and we arranged to meet at his home in Birsfilden near Basle. He seemed very pleased that we would meet at last, as we had been corresponding with each other for a long time. After Elinda's treatment at the Montreux Clinic was completed, we were driven to Birsfilden.

We stayed at a hotel near the Franks' home. Otto's second wife, Fritzi, was also a survivor of Auschwitz. She had lost her husband and son during the Holocaust, but survived together with her daughter Eva. Fritzi and Otto had a lot in common and they understood each other's grief.

Otto and his lovely wife Fritzi had made a warm and loving home together, and they made us feel very welcome. Otto was so touched by Elinda's condition that he had arranged for a specially-trained attendant to be present when we visited his house, so that she wouldn't become bored while we talked about the diary.

We discussed Otto's surprise at the depth of his daughter's diary, and its incredible effect on humanity. He was still receiving letters from all over the world. The diary, he said, had come so close to being destroyed but had miraculously been saved. After the Frank family was arrested, the diary was found on the floor of their attic by some office girls, who kept it in a drawer where they worked. They did not read its contents, as it was marked 'Private', and they hoped Anne would return to claim it. Had they read the diary, they would have been compelled to destroy it for their own safety because it proved that they had been helping those in hiding. For this crime they would have been severely punished, possibly even killed.

I was very touched when Otto gave me some of Anne's short stories – a gift I treasure to this day.

We took some photographs, and then Fritzi prepared a lovely lunch for all of us. It was an unforgettable day. When we finally left, Otto kissed us goodbye, then took out a big handkerchief and waved until we were out of sight. It remains one of my most treasured memories.

I found Otto Frank to be a dignified and true gentleman, with no hate in his heart. He asked me to keep in touch, and let him know Elinda benefited from her treatment. We continued our correspondence until Otto passed away in August of 1980 at the age of 91.

He had fulfilled his mission to bring Anne's diary to the attention of the world.

I kept in touch with Fritzi for a long time after Otto's death. At the age of 91 she left her Swiss home to live with her daughter and her family in London.

Anne Frank continued to influence my life.

In 1984, 'The Dairy of Anne Frank' was presented on stage again. Roger Climpson took the role of Anne's father.

Herman and I were invited to a performance and to meet the cast. I showed them all the information I had received from Otto Frank, letters, articles and pictures, and left them all with Roger. A few weeks later, he and his wife Claire came to our house to return the papers. Herman showed Roger the story that he had just finished writing about his own war experiences. At the back of the manuscript was a chapter about Elinda coming into our lives.

Roger was so touched with that chapter that he asked us if he could write her story. Both Herman and I agreed. Roger began to come to the house on a regular basis, to tape interviews with both of us. In that way he had a clear picture of everything that had happened since Elinda's birth.

Before we met Roger, Herman and I had found it very difficult to discuss Elinda's condition, as we had very different views on her treatment. At first, talking to Roger was very painful for both of us, as we had never really examined each other's point of view. All our buried emotions had to be brought out in the open, so that Roger could understand the situation as it had unfolded from the very beginning. By the time the book was finished, it had been a real healing experience for both of us. We had carried these burdens around for such a long time, always careful not to bring up our different outlooks, so as to avoid arguments.

Roger had a wonderful perception of the story and he understood both our points of view. In the process, the burdens were lifted from

Herman and I, and harmony re–established.

The book *Elinda* was published in 1987, by Hodder & Stoughton in Sydney. I will always be grateful to Roger for writing such an accurate and inspiring story of Elinda's purpose in coming into our lives.

I still receive cards and letters from people who have a child like Elinda. They write that they have found encouragement through reading *Elinda* and do not feel as isolated as before. Many households fall apart when a handicapped child comes into a family. Usually one of the two partners is less able to cope with the added stress than the other. Today, of course, there is a lot more help available for our handicapped children and their parents. When Elinda was born in 1958 no such support existed. I was looked upon with amazement and hostility by the medical profession, who thought I refused to accept the limitations of Down's Syndrome. They were wrong. What I

Herman and I with Roger Climpson. This photo was taken at Roger's home at the launch of the book Elinda, *1987.*

In front of the clinic in Switzerland, where I took Elinda for her cellular therapy, in 1969. My cousin Rebecca lived in Brussels, and she and her husband, Jo, came to pick us up after the treatment. Joe is taking the photo.

could not accept was their attitude of hopelessness.

I always felt that there was a purpose behind this ordeal and that I had to work through the situation to the best of my ability. To me it was a challenge, and it was absolutely natural to me to proceed in a positive manner. To see Elinda slowly become aware of her surroundings and begin to recognise the other members of her family was a great joy.

Now Elinda enjoys birthdays and family gatherings, and always loves the attention she gets as she demonstrates a new skill. She has a great sense of pride when she succeeds at something, all of which proves that children who may be intellectually disabled still have normal human responses. My intuition which recognised that fact was totally justified.

Since Herman is no longer with us, Elinda is good company for me, while providing me, as always, with a sense of purpose. God, indeed, works in mysterious ways.

'All my family was killed during the war... I was left to carry forth the family's source of life to continue the Journey...'

Most of the grandchildren: Maurits (four), Betty (two and a half), Zak (18 months), Klara (six and a half), Nini (four), Elizabeth (18 months), Claire (two and a half), Chellie (three). I was the only survivor.

CHAPTER SEVENTEEN

THE JOURNEY WITHIN

Because of the trials and tribulations I have suffered in my life, I have become even more receptive to an inner guidance. When Elinda was born, I needed to find the means to cope with life's traumas. I had to find out what life was about and most of all, the purpose behind our existence.

The gradual unfolding of consciousness led me to study and read books that would widen my horizons into a search for knowledge and a more purposeful life. I needed to know what was happening to me, when biblical passages were revealed to me by my inner guide. These stories came alive and clarified themselves. At first this was startling, especially as I had no knowledge of these subjects, and no interest in them.

I found in my search that the prophets of old had tried to convey the same messages to humanity, so many centuries ago.

We usually reach out for knowledge only when life's problems seem insurmountable, and we have nothing else to cling to in order to sustain ourselves in balance and harmony.

All my tribulations had brought me to the fringe of endurance, but it was the birth of Elinda that forced me to surrender into that 'presence' that is infinite by nature.

As human beings we are limited by our consciousness. In the learning process of my expanding awareness, there were periods of great joy and wonder. Here was a part of my life about which I had known nothing.

For a while it was almost as if I was living in two worlds, an inner universe of peace and harmony, and my everyday existence with all its ups and downs, but one thing I did know. My feet had to be firmly grounded and I had to live a balanced life in order to function practically. However, I was guided in whatever was needed to be done, not only to keep Elinda alive but to bring her to her full potential. I was steadfast in bringing that about.

In my studies I have learned that the prophets of old tried to convey a message that living our lives attuned to our inner resources would enable us to live in greater harmony and peace with our fellow human beings and ourselves.

As the inner meaning of their spiritual messages unfolded in my consciousness, life took on new challenges as I began to practise what I was learning from this deeper dimension. There was a sense of peace with me almost constantly, and I learned eventually to trust this higher source to lead the way. I learned also that I should literally 'let the Presence go before me to make the crooked places straight'.

Whatever the prophets of old had tried to teach humanity was universal and applicable to all men. There is no division in spiritual creation. God has no theology. Religions are primarily man–made concepts designed to dominate people. There seems to be very little love or grace involved.

Our spiritual resources lie deep in our innermost beings, in which we carry our complete pattern of creation and our divine heritage for a fruitful life on earth. In most of us, this lies dormant until that moment of readiness when we learn to reach out for it. We then will discover that our true selves contain the essence of pure creation that underlies all effect. This source contains no religious labels or divisions. It is a vibrant, living substance that knows its own destiny and forms its own pattern, in which like begets like. Without man's interference it is perfect and eternal.

Mankind divided humanity into different garments and creeds. Humanhood evolved when we accepted two powers, good and evil. (Who told you that you were naked?) In some religions this is termed the Fall of Man, which really means the acceptance of the sense of creation as the only reality. Instead, we must realise that the 'pattern shown thee on the Mount' is the blueprint of eternal creation. This is what each of us carries in our individual consciousness, and it is our birthright. Man has been given dominion over his affairs, and only our ignorance of this fact keeps us from its benefits.

Instead we devise religions, build places of worship and develop sects, and all these chaotic divisions bring with them hatred, conflict and wars, pushing people to the brink of their own destruction.

Our roots are in the pure essence of Creation, and this must be acknowledged by each individual, but we must also let the false concepts of life dissolve, so that the reality of Creation can be experienced. Only then can we reach that state of fulfilment that was intended for us on Earth. Life is a journey in consciousness that must be undertaken individually. We must free ourselves of the conditioned mind that has for centuries believed that there are either superior or inferior races on earth established by our Creator. None of this man-made nonsense was meant to be.

Every soul on Earth has its place and is a link in a Creation that would otherwise be incomplete. Only when we have learned these lessons of tolerance and equality will we bring forth the Brotherhood of Man, in which the lamb and the lion will be at peace together.

The greatest blessing I have received during my life's journey is the inner assurance that life is eternal. What we call 'death' is merely the end of the physical journey. We continue on to express our existence on a different level of life. This is a natural process of unfolding consciousness. We leave our physical body behind because we have no use for that vehicle on the next stage of our journey. Our enduring consciousness provides the only vehicle we require for the next experience.

There is an all-knowing Creator at work and we cannot interfere with the harmony of His eternal plan, which includes the sanctity of human life. This means that no-one has the right to take the life of another. Each of us is unique and each of us is needed to complete the infinite circle of Creation. Unless we respect all life on earth unconditionally, we must return until we learn to do so. Only then are we motivated to serve the Universe.

My children, Martin, Elinda, and Jerry.

CHAPTER EIGHTEEN

LIVING WITH MEMORIES

Our two sons were growing up and we had every reason to be proud of them. Martin and Jerry made friends easily, and both were prefects at high school. They were both sports-minded, just as Herman and I had been, and played golf and tennis. Martin also played soccer, and represented Australia with his high school team in 1962-64, and also later on with his club team.

Jerry was also a good soccer player, and coached soccer teams.

Being a keen fan, Herman never missed a game, and this gave him a healthy outlet for his inner struggles. Whenever possible, he took Elinda with him to watch her brothers, and to this day Elinda loves ball games.

Jerry became a recreational officer with the Ministry of Sport, and worked for six years at the University of New South Wales in this profession. Martin became a successful businessman. It made us feel wonderful to see the boys grow up into such balanced and down-to-earth young men.

Elinda was enrolled in the kindergarten of the Windgap Special School, and at the Windgap Activity Centre, where she still goes daily.

Our three children continue to have a close and loving relationship.

Herman still could not bear to talk about the horrors of his past, and we seldom talked about these experiences openly with each other. The thawing out process was especially painful for Herman, whose artistic temperament was very sensitive and really craved harmony. I don't think he could bear to think about the cruelties inflicted upon his family, friends and those others who did not come home. He became more and more involved with Elinda and that also helped to divert his mind.

He would not go on holiday without taking Elinda, and when we travelled overseas she always came with us. As for me, I knew that I had to learn to survive my memories in order to carry on. If it had not been for Elinda, I would not have found the means to draw on my inner resources for strength and, in the process, learn about the meaning of life. I became aware of just how difficult it is for most people to find a reason for their problems and still continue with their everyday lives.

In 1971 Martin met Leonie, and not long after they became engaged. They married a year later. Our first grandchild, Nicole Claire, was born four years later.

The joy Herman and I felt as grandparents was very special, and we were overcome with gratitude. When their second child, Nathan David, was born, Martin and Leonie felt their family was complete.

Who would have thought Herman and I would live to know such joy? We had again established a family circle.

By this time Jerry had met his future wife, Ingeborg, and after a short engagement they married. We now had two lovely daughters-in-law, and soon the added joy of two more grandchildren, Daniel Aaron and Tamara Michelle.

To watch children grow and develop is a continuing blessing, all part of establishing a family clan and something that brought healing to both of us, but we were careful never to take these events for granted. We had been too close to being wiped off the Earth.

As time went on we continued our family get-togethers and every Friday night we would have the traditional family dinner at our home. That was a link to our past, as we all felt the special meaning of being able to celebrate the Sabbath meal and give thanks for the love and joy that brought us together as a family.

I particularly remember, when I was in the darkness of despair during the war years, that the thought of our joyful family celebrations gave me strength. The family life I once had was like a protective shield around me. No one could take that part of my life away from me.

I reflected often on the incredible journey I had undertaken in this lifetime. I naturally became fascinated by the different philosophies of life and attended lectures and courses on the subject as often as I could. I am an avid reader, but mostly I live by my own intuition, and this led to having people turn to me, those who were beset by their own problems.

I know only too well the value of helping wherever I can. There were many times when I myself really needed a helping hand to lift me out of my sorrows, but one was not available. Most of the time, I had to struggle on my own.

I cannot help reflecting on what is happening in the world today and wonder if we have learned nothing from all the past horrors in our history. However, there is an optimistic flame within me that compels me to be positive on the final outcome for the world being good. That is its destiny. And fortunately, this is in the hand of God, and not dependent on evil doers.

We must recognise that we are responsible for our actions and our conduct towards our fellow human beings. We cannot hide behind a facade of ignorance and blame other influences for the cruelties we inflict on our fellow human beings.

The fact that the Nazi regime concocted their warped plan for the total annihilation of Europe's Jewish people is beyond doubt. The sad truth is that they found people willing to carry out their evil intentions. Without that assistance their plans could not have been realised, and this should not be forgotten. These crimes against humanity were frequently committed by educated people – doctors, teachers, lawyers, judges, generals. This makes their crimes even more hideous, for they offend civilisation and of course their professions. Many of their victims were fooled by these creatures' civilised appearance, but their merciless conduct was worse than that of beasts.

Any form of race discrimination is evil, as there is a purpose in God's creation for every individual, otherwise they would not be on earth.

I feel that it is particularly important we educate our children about our common heritage, so that feelings of division or difference can be eradicated before they take hold. Unfortunately, many people have grown up with discrimination as the norm, and find it rather natural to behave in this way.

One of the reasons that the survivors of the Holocaust have to remind people about the horrors they endured, is that for centuries the Jewish people have been victimised by prejudice and blamed for whatever was wrong in society. Even at Auschwitz I remember many victims saying, 'Well, if this is what it means to be God's chosen people, it is about time someone else was chosen.'

No one can float to heaven on someone else's back, or get there by denigrating other people, and the sooner we, as humanity, accept that fact, the happier we may be. By trying to destroy others we destroy ourselves – a principle we have not yet learned, here on Earth. Enduring peace can never be achieved by going to war, but by recognising the equality of all men on Earth.

In our innermost being we share one consciousness and our basic needs are the same. I feel that the diversity of races, colours and nationalities on this Earthly plane was created to teach us the lessons of tolerance and understanding.

I have witnessed the most unbearable degradations that man can inflict on other human beings. I have also witnessed, among the many victims, the beauty and divinity of the human soul that refused to allow them to become like beasts in the field, that refused to let them yield to their tormentors. Their spirits could not be broken. To survive in Auschwitz took every ounce of mental and physical endurance and strength that one could muster.

I have, of course, haunting memories of prisoners who knew that their time was up, who had been 'selected ' to go to the gas chamber that very day. They looked at us and said, 'You will tell the world what took place here.' Of course, we did not think that anyone of us would survive to tell the tale, but we promised them anyway, that we would carry out their last request.

In 1995, half a century later, I was given a unique opportunity to honour that promise. I received a telephone call from a survivor friend, who asked if I wanted to participate in a project set up by Steven Spielberg, the director of 'Schindler's List', for a film about the Holocaust. His work with survivors of the Holocaust had affected him deeply, and he now wanted to do something to preserve eyewitness accounts of the victims of the Holocaust. He set up a foundation that would videotape interviews with survivors about their individual experiences. These tapes would form a permanent record and be used in educational and historic projects to teach future generations the truth about the Holocaust.

I agreed to take part, and was interviewed for over three hours on video. A copy of the tape was later sent to me. Although in many ways a harrowing experience, it was a rewarding task, because my testimony was now recorded for all time. For many survivors this interview was a healing process. It was, and still is, difficult for survivors to relate the specific details of their concentration camp terrors and torment. After their interviews, many are on record as saying that they felt a great sense of release.

In my innermost being I embrace all my companions who lost their lives during the Holocaust. I feel such a close bond with all those who had to take that journey through the Valley of Death.

As I think of the incredible madness of the Nazi mind, I recall one incident that stood out among all the other atrocities for its sheer perversity.

One Sunday, we were told we would not have to go to work that day. During the afternoon we were pushed out of our hut and ordered to line up in rows of five. We then had to march to another hut in the camp. We were very tense, and couldn't imagine what was going to happen to us. We filed into the hut and there was the camp orchestra assembled. We stood in rows of five, waiting, and suddenly they started to play.

The contrast of music and the horrors that surrounded us was so incredibly painful, that many women burst into tears. On one side of the camp, the crematorium was burning, and only a few yards away the orchestra was playing! It was a truly heartbreaking experience, and I was so relieved when we left the hut.

I recall another morning, coming back to the camp after work at the munitions factory. We were told to remain outside as we had to be seen by the doctors. A state of panic broke out among the prisoners. What did the SS have in mind this time? We had no choice, however, but to comply, as orders were given at gunpoint. We marched in and filed one by one past the doctors and prison warders. Each of us received an injection in the arm. You can imagine how tense we were, waiting to see who among us would survive. So often this was a method of execution. To this day, I don't know what was injected into my arm.

Yet I struggled on day by day.

In early June of 1944, a transport arrived from Holland. When I heard about its arrival, I set out to smuggle myself into the quarantine block, so that I could speak to the young women who had just come. They were so full of optimism. They said that the Allies had landed in Europe on the 6th of June.

I said nothing.

The transports from Hungary had just started to arrive and the lines of people waiting to go into the gas chambers were endless. I later heard that from July of 1944 to October of that year, only three months, between 450 000–500 000 Hungarian Jews were eliminated. We lived in a haze of smoke and dust from the burning corpses.

SS Colonel Eichmann was the instigator of this carnage. He was relentless in his pursuit of his iniquitous Final Solution. In 1960 Eichmann was kidnapped from his hiding place in Argentina, and taken to Israel to be put on trial for his crimes.

His defence was that he had 'acted under orders'.

After a long and fair trial, he was found guilty and hanged in 1962.

In the autumn of 1944 the Union squad was moved from Birkenau to Auschwitz women's camp, and our living conditions improved to a certain extent. The barracks were clean and the facilities inside were more comfortable. Also, we were further away from the railroad, so we did not have to watch transports of prisoners arriving from the occupied countries, on their way to the crematorium.

This was the camp that housed the notorious barrack where medical experiments were carried out on women. These women were sometimes seen out in the courtyard, walking around behind the barbed wire that separated them from the other inmates. Among them I discovered a number of women that I had known from Amsterdam, and some from my gymnastic club. As long as the experiments lasted, these women were kept in reasonably clean conditions, but they suffered agonies while the experiments were carried out. In addition, they lived in a state of constant suspense, as many died in that barrack.

In the first half of January, 1945, rumours started to filter into the camp that the Russians were getting closer. We could hear cannon fire in the distance, but we also knew that the Germans would never let us be liberated. On the day we were to be evacuated from Auschwitz, I was called out by the *Kapo* of our block.

She said, 'Someone wants to see you at the gate. You will go with a warder.'

I could not imagine what this was about but had no say in the matter.

When we arrived at the gate, I saw a prisoner standing on the other side, with a guard at his side. When I had a closer look, I saw he was a political non-Jewish inmate by the name of Marius van der Sluys.

He had belonged to the Dutch Resistance group *Geusen* (Giants), but had been denounced and sent to the most notorious camps. He spoke to me in Dutch and said, 'We will be marching out tonight. All I could find for you is a packet of honey. Remain at the head of the group. They won't leave you behind if you can't walk. Stragglers will be shot. I know because I have already been on a march, from Warsaw to Auschwitz. Be strong and keep going. Good luck.'

Our little group of women lived on that packet of honey for a number of days, and Marius' advice probably helped to save our lives.

Many years after the war, I was delighted to find out that not only had Marius survived the death march, but he had been decorated by the Dutch government for his bravery during the war. Marius lived to a great age and was in his nineties when he died.

In 1947 I received a message from an earlier gallant saviour, Jo Panke, our Resistance friend who had helped us to reach Belgium.

He had heard that Herman and I had both survived the camps and wanted to visit us to tell us what had happened after his arrest. We were also told that he was not well and needed to say his farewells to us.

When he arrived at our home, he was on crutches and supported by his priest. We were shocked to see him in such a debilitated state, indeed, we could barely recognise him, for his face was misshapen and swollen.

We both cried.

So did he.

Then he told us his story. Shortly before I was arrested Jo had been denounced by people we both knew. Jo had helped so many people escape, and these people denounced him after they themselves had been arrested. Jo was tortured and beaten so viciously that he almost died. He was put into a concentration camp at Vucht in the Netherlands, where he lived in the constant expectation that he would be shot. However, the camp was in the southern part of Holland and liberated by the Allies in 1944. Jo was freed, but he was very close to death.

He was hospitalised, where it was discovered that he had developed cancer of the face, as a result of the vicious beatings he had suffered. When he was told the truth about his diagnosis, he sought us out to say 'Goodbye'.

He died a short time later.

After the war, the people who had denounced him were imprisoned by the Belgian government. Herman and I attended their trial to give evidence against them.

What inspired us over the years was the knowledge that there were people like Jo Panke, people who stepped forward and courageously defied the evildoers. We had the great good fortune of meeting some of these people. I endlessly salute those brave souls, who have made our life's journey lighter.

There is no clear–cut answer to the question, 'Why did you survive when so many did not?' Of course, destiny had to provide witnesses, so that the truth could be reported to the world. Some people seem to think that the Holocaust should be forgotten and put aside. That would of course forfeit the purpose of the development of civilisation. As long as there is bestiality in the mind of man, it will have to be exposed. It cannot remain hidden. We must deal with it, so that there is no room left for deception. We cannot remain ignorant of the evil of which men are capable. This is all part of our learning experience.

Herman during a session for Sydney radio station 2UW

CHAPTER NINETEEN

HERMAN

Almost imperceptibly, Herman's health began to deteriorate. He did not want to draw attention to his ill–health, but when his breathing became difficult we often had to rush him to the Emergency Department of the Prince of Wales Hospital.

He finally consulted a cardiologist, who put him through a series of tests and discovered that he had a leaking heart valve. The specialist thought that Herman must have suffered some infection during his imprisonment. Of course, the infection was never treated in the camps, where the only cure for illness was death.

Herman was put on medication for his condition. He was told an operation would eventually be essential, when a replacement heart valve would be inserted. By 1990 it had become obvious that Herman could wait no longer, and so he underwent an operation to repair his heart. Unfortunately, he never really recovered from that operation. His other organs started to fail, but he never gave way to gloom.

Three weeks before he passed on, he suddenly said to me, 'Well, I think this is it.'

On the 4th of August, 1991, Herman passed away at St Luke's Hospital, where Elinda had been born on the 25th of June in 1958. The 4th of August was also the day when the Frank family had been arrested in 1944.

The day before Herman died, I was sitting by his bedside with Jerry. Herman suddenly sat up without saying a word. He looked at me rather sadly and embraced me. He held onto me for a while, before he lay down again and closed his eyes. I thought, 'Oh, Herman, you are saying goodbye.'

The next day he passed away peacefully.

During the last few months of his life, Herman often reflected on his survival. What gave him satisfaction was that Hitler had not succeeded in entirely wiping his family from the earth. He was so grateful that his family line could live on through his children and grandchildren. That one thing had given his survival meaning.

I often look around at his many paintings which fill our home, and I am forever grateful that he found a way of expressing the creativity of his soul. He often said, 'Through my music and art, I have been blessed with the opportunity to connect with the beauty of life again.'

Herman's passing was very difficult for Elinda to accept. At first she did not cope very well, and frequently cried. She was very attached to her father, and suddenly he was not in her life any more. I found it hard to explain to her what had happened and hoped that time would take care of the situation for her.

I would like to mention here something that happened the year before Herman left us. For a number of years Elinda had refused to

Herman and Sam, 1978

Department of Defence

Record Office

The Hague 9th April 1975
Hooftskade 1

Statement

This is certify that:

- - - - - - - - - - **L I S S I N G**, Herman - - - - - - - - - -
born on 27th November 1919 at Amsterdam (the Netherlands), army-number 19.11.27.017. was on active service as a private with the Royal Netherlands Ground Forces - 3th Regiment Air Forces - in the rank of a sergeant during the following periods:
from 5th June 1939 till 29th June 1940 and
from 23th January 1947 till 2th November 1947.
During the war-days of May 1940 he actually served in the Theatre of war.
With entrance from 1st Oktober 1959 he was discharged because of ending military service.

Chief Record Office of the
Department of Defence.,

(M.J.van Druten)

Requested by: himself
By letter of 24th March 1975

speak outside the house. We tried all we could to encourage her to speak, but nothing worked.

Shortly after Herman's operation he was in intensive care. I went to get Elinda from school to take her to visit him. On the way to the hospital I said to her, 'Elinda, when you see Daddy, please say "Hello Daddy" in a loud voice. That would make him very happy.'

I gave it no further thought, but when we entered his hospital room, Elinda suddenly called out loudly, 'Hello Daddy. I am Elinda.'

Even though Herman was only semi–conscious, he smiled broadly in delight. From that day, Elinda has spoken normally wherever she goes. Her refusal to speak outside the house dissolved on that day. I am so grateful that Herman was able to experience that joy before he passed on. Elinda's silence had distressed him, as he felt she was capable of speech in any situation. Later Herman said to me, 'If it took my illness to make her speak in public, it was worth it.'

It took Elinda a whole year to adjust to life without her father. She has now accepted his absence, and when she is asked, 'Where is Daddy?' she answers, 'Daddy is with God.' We all miss Herman very much, but we know he is at peace. Elinda is healthy and has improved generally. We continue our lives together, in the midst of a loving and supportive family.

Herman and I, in February 1983

EPILOGUE

JERRY'S RECOLLECTIONS

One of my earliest memories as a child was of sitting on my mother's lap and looking at some strange blue numbers written on her arm.

I remember asking mum what they were. She told me they were her old telephone number, and that satisfied me, at least for a while.

My recollections of early childhood are generally that of a happy, carefree life with Mum, Dad and big brother Martin. I recall with great clarity the news that mum was going to have a baby and how happy we all were—fun-filled days in Maroubra, going to the soccer, the excitement of getting our first TV!

Mum did get very ill while she was pregnant and I remember her crying a lot. I thought it must be because she was ill yet there was something more. Dad worked long hours and I would wait for the comforting smell of the tobacco from his pipe or cigar preceding him as he came up the front path. He was a great dad and he loved us but he was, I guess, restless, not quite happy.

When our sister Elinda was born, Martin and I were told she was very sick and couldn't come home for a while. I did perceive at that time that my mother somehow gained an inner strength and a quiet determination. Why? I didn't know, but it somehow made everything seem all right. There were times when the hushed, tense conversation of my parents in a language I couldn't quite understand, made it seem as though they were hiding something—a secret we weren't supposed to know about.

I never spoke about it to my brother or my parents as I felt they were, in their way, protecting me.

As I grew older I noticed my mother was writing a lot. As she sat at the kitchen table, I joined her and asked her what she was doing. Ever so slowly I learned that I didn't have grandparents because they were 'killed in the war'. I found out that bad things had happened to the Jewish people and that my parents were somehow involved.

I didn't find this out all at once—it was a gradual revelation that I came to through conversations with my friends who were also children of survivors, through the television and through snippets of hushed conversations—but I eventually discovered that Jews were put in camps and killed by the Nazis.

I appreciated the fact that whenever I asked my parents a question they answered me in a way I could understand. They never dramatised or became uncontrollably emotional. The careful and loving way in which the stories of their lives and our family who perished were unfolded to us made these horrible events somehow seem an integral part of our family story. As unnatural and horrific as these events were, they set me personally on a path that I am still following. I don't know where it's going but I am drawn to a destination that is somehow linked to my family's past. My journey is manifesting itself as a duty and perhaps a mission that I haven't yet fulfilled.

My own family is more precious to me as a result of my parents' experiences. We were meant to be together. I have a bond with my brother and sister that is very strong. I feel very close to them and love who they are. My sister is so much more than meets the eye. She is a whole person and a blessing that helped my parents focus on their future and made all of us more compassionate.

I really didn't feel any great sense of loss until I got to know my extended family through my parents. My loving upbringing, friends and sports have helped me enjoy my life and cope with the memories transferred to me by stories and photos.

I am happy my father found peace in his last years, that he faced his inner demons and conquered them.

My mother has given me more than I can express. Her gift of

purpose and compassion for others I endeavour to bring into every facet of my life and I will pass this, as a legacy from our beloved family, to my children.

In 1971 Martin met Leonie, and not long after they became engaged. They married a year later.

With my first granddaughter, Martin and Leonie's daughter Nicole, at eighteen months.

Martin and Leonie's son Nathan, at 3.

Jerry and Ingeborg's children, Daniel at 3 years of age and his younger sister Tamara, 2.

Me and Nathan, my grandson in the Australian Army, prior to his deployment to East Timor as a U.N. Peacekeeper.

A FINAL WORD

It was not long after my liberation from the death camp that I started to record events that had taken place in Auschwitz and similar camps. Many survivors keep the painful memories of their experiences buried within their consciousness, finding them too traumatic to recall, and indeed, it is difficult to put on paper the details of life in Auschwitz. How can one describe the shock one felt on entering the camp, to find out that people were being gassed and burned in the ovens?

These people's only crime was to be born Jewish. You become aware that all those people you loved and cherished and shared your life with are being eliminated by that process. The struggle for personal survival begins as soon as you enter the camp. There is no time to absorb the horrors because you realise you may not be alive even an hour from the present moment.

No prisoner that entered Auschwitz was prepared for the bestiality, the murderous regime practised in this destruction camp. One simply could not fathom that the human species could perpetrate such evil. The SS had represented the lowest denomination of life on Earth. They had no capacity for mercy in their system – they even took delight in killing defenceless babies and elderly people. As a matter of fact, murder was their favourite pastime and their training was concentrated on that activity. Having experienced the conditions that existed in the various concentration camps it was almost a comfort to know that the people you loved so much had died on their arrival rather that first being exposed to life inside the camps.

This was a shocking realisation for me, but that is the truth as I see it. Herman felt the same way, because we both knew so many prisoners, who died there, after having been exposed to the cruel camp conditions first. What I have always thought miraculous is that most of the survivors I know have managed to put their lives back on track.

The pain remains, but the real values of family life and common decency have prevailed. When people returned home again they endeavoured to become members of a normal society and instill in their children the values they themselves had known before the tragedy.

Throughout all my trials and tribulations I refused to allow the misery of Auschwitz to deprive me of my dignity. If only my physical body were to survived, my survival would have been in vain.

I could never forget a girl in Auschwitz who knew she was about to be gassed. She looked me in the face and said, 'Well, good, I know what they are after. They want my life destroyed but I will stay in charge of myself. I was given my life by God and I will surrender my life back to God. They do not possess me.' In the final moments of her life on earth she freed herself from the clutches of the Nazis. She triumphed over her tormentors. The physical body can be destroyed, but its life belongs to God and continues to live in His light.

The learning process continues and the lessons we have absorbed remain with us.

I recall my second day in Auschwitz, standing at rollcall and looking out on the snow–covered, muddy ground. I remember seeing what appeared to be pieces of wood lying on the ground near the barracks. After rollcall was over, I walked near some of these huts and froze to the spot. These pieces of wood were the dead bodies of the women who had died overnight.

This was a regular sight at Auschwitz. At first I was in a state of disbelief, but later I became immune to the situation. Another regular sight was the daily suicide of prisoners throwing themselves at the highpowered fence surrounding the campsite – instant death for those who could take no more. Then there were the nights our work command walked from the campsite to the munition factory to begin our nightshift work. Many nights we were overtaken by trucks on their way to the gas chambers. They were full of naked men, all singing the 'Hatikvah', the song of hope. These men had been selected during the day to be exterminated that same night, simply to make more room for new arrivals from the German–occupied countries.

It took all those long years after my liberation from the death camps to write down the full Auschwitz experience as I remembered it. To my beloved companions who perished there, I can honestly say, I have told your story and mine. I promised you I would but it took some courage to recall the misery. I always knew I had to do it one day while I could still muster the strength for it.

It is a promise fulfilled now.

Somewhere there is a meaning to this incredible horror. The lessons to be learned from such a tragedy are for those that stay behind. We set in motion the cause and its effect is the natural result of the act we carry out. Good rewards itself, evil creates its return. In the end, what we do to others bounces back. This is the law of creation. If we want evil to stop on the earth, we individually have to refuse to express it. There is no other way. This is Man's responsibility. God has given us our free will to choose our path. It is the source of the destiny that made us survive that edges us on to reveal to the world the fate of those that did not survive.

I, for one, felt that our ignorance of the potential for evil that exists within some contributed to the slaughter of millions. I also know that hate and prejudice are still rampant in the world at large.

We are searching outer space to discover other planets we can inhabit, but our number one priority should be to find peace and tolerance here on Earth. Otherwise, what contribution can we make to the universe? We will not have peace until we have developed a consciousness of peace.

The material in this book came together over a period of 40 years.

The first ten years after my liberation from the death camps were spent in a haze of pain and anguish realising the extent and brutality of the Nazi regime.

The most excruciating pain was caused by the loss of my beloved family and friends, at the hands of Hitler's henchmen. I felt bereft beyond belief and crushed by the knowledge of the way in which these people were murdered.

My personal traumas were suppressed as much as possible, but the time spent in these death camps took their toll and resulted in years of nightmares.

Herman, my husband, was unable ever to come to terms with the horrors he experienced and he put a shutter over his memories, so that he could go on living some form of a normal life. A gifted artist and musician, Herman found solace in his painting and music. It would be our Down's Syndrome daughter, Elinda, who would finally break down his barriers.

Our decision to move to Australia was a positive step that enabled us to begin again. Our children provided us with a new lease of life, and hope for the future. It was not always easy to explain to

Daniel, Tamara, Betty, Nicole and Nathan

our growing children why they had no grandparents or extended family in their lives. But we were grateful that we could provide them with love and care, and that we succeeded in making them respected members of society, without malice or hate for their fellow human beings.

Elinda and I continue to live in a positive way and are forever hopeful that humanity will develop a world in which people find no need to dominate others, and respect the right of an individual to live in peace.

I had been urged for many years to write my story, but I always felt that the time was not yet right, and my story incomplete. One morning, however, when I woke up I felt the urge to sit down and write a few pages. At the top of the page, I wrote 'God Cried at Auschwitz', then came the whole explanation of why that was so.

I had no preconceived idea about the subject, but the words tumbled forth and I felt a great sense of relief. Perhaps this was the answer to the burning question that has plagued humanity ever since – Where was God at Auschwitz? When I read what I had written to my son, Jerry, he said, 'That is the Foreword to your book.'

I had no choice but to write it.

"Have we not all one Father?"

—Malachi Chapter 2 verse 10.

During the war years we lost all our possessions, including our treasured photographs. However, Herman had an aunt by marriage who was not Jewish, and she was able to keep copies of some of our most cherished photographs of our family and our wedding day. I feel blessed that she could save them. Many are reproduced in this book.